Free Online High Schools

Earn your high school diploma for free

Thomas Nixon, M.A.

Degree Press
Fresno, California

Free Online High Schools
By Thomas Nixon

Copyright © 2015 by Thomas Nixon

Degree Press
4073 W. Cortland Avenue
Fresno, CA 93722
info@DegreePress.com

Warning: The author has attempted to accurately portray each school. However, the author will gladly post corrections on his website located at BestOnlineHighSchools.com or make corrections in the next edition of the book. Please send corrections to tom@thomasnixon.com.

To Elizabeth,

And

To Sarah, David, and Maria

Table of Contents

Chapter 1: Free Online High Schools

This is the first time in history that the teacher, student, and content do not have to be in the same place.

--Willard Daggett, President, International Center for Leadership in Education

Is there really enough information on free online high schools to write an entire book on the subject? Apparently so. Online high schools have been growing by a significant number over the last decade. Nowhere is that more evident than with the number of free versions of these schools.

While there have been online high schools around, in some form, for quite some time, over the last decade, the numbers of these schools has exploded. There are a number of reasons for why this has happened, but it really falls into three groups:

- Homeschoolers who want to use digital content;

- Students who need an alternative location due to interests in sports or visual/performing arts; or

- Students and families who have concerns about the traditional public school system.

That being said, there are as many reasons for wanting an online education as there are people seeking one.

Online high schools are becoming the schools of choice for a diverse population of students. For some, they provide a way out of traditional high schools and for others they offer a second chance at earning a diploma. Whatever the reason, online programs can be a convenient and sensible solution for many students. However, it is not necessarily an easy task to determine which are good choices and which are not.

And, should you have any doubt, making the right choice is the difference between a piece of paper that is worth something and one that is not. All things being equal, and in this case they must be, it is much better to choose carefully.

How you go about selecting an online high school can depend significantly on what your ultimate goal might be. While there are many possible goals, they tend to break down into two distinct choices:

- You wish to earn a high school diploma to improve your chances at getting a job or entering the military (see Chapter 2). College, at this point, is not something you are actively considering; or

- You wish to attend a college and you either feel the need or it is a stated requirement that you first earn a high school diploma.

Certainly both are valid reasons for considering earning a high school diploma online.

Different Free Options

There are several different types of free online high schools including:

- Public online charter schools
- School-district-sponsored online schools
- State-sponsored online schools

Public online charter schools are growing in number. Being a charter school, they have fewer rules to follow, but are still considered public schools (so, by law, must be free). These schools are typically quite small.

School-district-sponsored online schools can offer full-time and/or part-time programs.

A few states have developed their own online high schools. These school are primarily to offer courses that are not readily available to rural and inner city districts such as Advanced Placement and foreign language courses.

How do you choose a school?

Whatever the reason, choosing a school requires that you look at a number of criteria. The criteria below are the minimum acceptable standards for selecting an online high school:

- The school should be accredited by a regional or national accreditor recognized by the Council on Higher Education Accreditation or by the U.S. Department of Education. Other possible recognition includes that from state departments of education and public school districts.

- For full-time schools, there is a marked preference for schools to have been in operation for at least two years. That being said, what is more important is that the system or district has experience offering high school courses.

- You should be able to determine through its website or printed materials who owns and/or operates the school. This should include the names of employees such as the principal or other administrators.

- It should have printed materials. While this may seem simplistic, schools that have printed materials tend to be more established and much less likely to be a poor choice. It may be that those printed materials are downloadable in PDF format.

As has been explained, these are minimum requirements. If you have questions about specific schools, posting a question or two at BestOnlineHighSchools.com is a good place to start.

What does it take to be successful?

After determining whether it is a good choice in general, you should also determine if it is a good choice for you and whether you are a good choice for online learning.

The first place to start is to determine if you are an independent worker. It takes more dedication to complete an online course than it does to complete a traditional classroom-based course. If you are not able to work independently, you are opening yourself up to a major challenge.

Online courses come in two basic formats: limited time and less-limited time. In other words, some courses are structured within traditional quarters or semesters, while the completion date for others is farther in the future. Neither is better than the other, but understanding your own learning style can help you make better choices with regard to time.

If you find that you work better when you have very specific deadlines, a more traditional schedule likely works best for you. However, if you like things to be more open-ended or there is the possibility that you might need extra time, you should consider that second option. Be careful with that second option, though, because this can be one of the ways that students never finish their courses.

As mentioned before, online courses require real dedication to finish. How can you know if you are able to do this? Take a look at what you have accomplished in your life. Have you ever:

- worked for yourself? The same skills that are required to be your own boss are what are required to be a successful online student.

- completed tasks on a regular basis without being asked? The key component there is "...without being asked."

What are some other possibilities? Climbing a mountain is a good metaphor for what you will need to endure. You get the idea. You can be successful if you have not done these sorts of things, but it certainly makes it all that much harder.

The Role of Family Support

If you find yourself lacking in the skills necessary to be a good online candidate, all is not lost. Many of the more successful online learners rely on their families, whether that is parents or spouse, to provide them with the necessary support to be successful. Sometimes all it takes is asking for the extra help.

Chapter 2: Frequently Asked Questions

The future of online learning is clearly one of increased usage by all sectors of education, kindergarten through postgraduate study.

--Michael Lambert, executive director, Distance Education & Training Council

Asking the right questions is your first step on the road to being an online school student. Knowing the right questions to ask can be problematic.

The questions answered below are a beginning, but you will want to ask many more questions of potential online schools. It is a very good idea to get as much information on a variety of schools before making your decision.

Why should I consider an online school?

Online schools can be a good choice for several reasons. If you are an older student, you may not wish to go to a traditional adult school. By earning the diploma online, you have a mask of anonymity that may protect your self-esteem.

Another possibility is that traditional high school may not be working out for you or for your child. Perhaps your child goes to a "less than wonderful" school that does not provide enough opportunities for success. Perhaps your child is having social issues with other students that necessitates leaving the school.

An additional possibility is the advantage for learning-challenged students. If you or your child requires more processing time, more time to read, or other accommodations, an online school could be a good choice. While time is not unlimited, you certainly have more available than from your local public school.

Will it help me get into the military?

The answer has recently changed. Online schools used to be classified as Tier 2 for military acceptance. This meant that they were less desirable, but might be acceptable depending on certain factors such as slots available. Tier 2 also includes the GED.

However, all that has changed, and online school diplomas were moved to Tier 1 in 2012. This puts them on the same level as any other high school diploma out there. It should be no more challenging for you to enlist in the military than for someone who went to a traditional high school.

Why is it important to choose an accredited high schools?

There are a couple of reasons for selecting an accredited online school. Accreditation ensures you of a minimum level of education. It does not mean that you are guaranteed to get a high-quality education. It will, however, give you an acceptable minimum level.

The other and equally important reason is the acceptability of the diploma itself. A university will accept almost all regionally-accredited high school diplomas, many nationally-accredited ones, and an indeterminate number from unaccredited schools. It is that indetermination that is the problem. The perception is that most unaccredited schools are unaccredited because they do not meet that minimum level. Whether that is true or not is not particularly important. The reality is the perception of those schools.

In a marked change from 2007, it has become clear that recognition by state departments of education and public school districts also have much value. One note, though, is to ensure that the state recognition comes from the department of education and nowhere else. Some states do provide recognition, but it is more of a consumer awareness process and does not attest to the educational quality and often comes from a different department.

Are online schools easier than traditional schools?

It is almost certain that some online schools are easier than some traditional schools. Guess what? California State University, Fresno is easier than Harvard University. Some schools are easier and some are more difficult. This is the nature of education.

Having said that, students typically find online schools more challenging than traditional ones. At traditional schools, you have teachers that will follow up with you and make sure you are turning in assignments. You are also required to be in a certain place at a certain time every day. The same cannot be said about online courses.

Online students need to have more internal motivation. You need to be the sort of person that can get the job done independently. If you are not, that online school experience most assuredly will not be easier than that traditional experience.

How much do online schools cost?

While some online schools are expensive, more than $10,000 per year, others are absolutely free. While cost alone should not determine your choice, it would be foolish to believe that cost is not a determining factor in the selection process.

However, one thing to bear in mind is that the amount of transferable credits from your old high school to your new one can vary widely. While the cost may be more at one school, it might also accept more of your credits. Determining which is the best deal in terms of cost means you need to do your research.

However, if you live in an area that has free online school programs, all bets are off. That is almost always your best choice. Free really is the best price. You should still do your homework, though, because you may discover that you can finish sooner by paying fees to that other school.

Where are those free online schools located?

Just a few short years ago, there were very few free online schools. With the explosion of charter schools in the 2000s, the number of free online options grew rapidly.

In 2007, a guess was made that the number of such schools would "...continue to grow." There is no doubt that this has come to pass. Many communities now have a local option available. No, they are still not in all states, but certainly in many.

I do not live in an area that has free online schools. Are there less expensive options?

If a free online school is not in your future, it is important to remember that the world is then your oyster. You can go to school anywhere that you choose. While the free schools tie you down geographically, when that is not an option for you, then you can choose a school that is across the country or down the street.

The difference in cost between schools can hinge upon how many of your previous high school credits are accepted at each school. You could find schools that will accept none of those credits and others that will accept all of them.

Are there age requirements?

Some schools do have a maximum age limit, often around the traditional age for high school graduation. Others will accept students up to the age of 21. Still others, have none whatsoever.

Many of the private schools, the commercial programs like Penn Foster High School, allow students of all ages. Other private schools, like Laurel Springs School, are for traditional-aged students.

Where age commonly becomes a factor is in the public programs whether that is a public charter school or an online school attached to a school district.

For many programs, though, there is no age requirement. I have heard often that the reason why someone has chosen to go back and earn a diploma online instead of in a traditional classroom is precisely because they do not want to be with traditional-aged high school students. Nothing wrong with that; if you are thirty-five, you just may not want to take classes with someone who is seventeen (and, likely, they do not want to take classes with you!). That is one of the nice things about online schools; there are many choices and one of those choices is age.

What about all of these high school diplomas through testing programs that I see on the Internet?

Unfortunately, they are scams. The only legitimate way to earn a high school diploma through testing is a program like the California High School Proficiency Exam (CHSPE). Note that this is a program of the State of California's Department of Education. Interestingly, this is a very common question. People often want the easy way out and it seems a reasonable sort of thing. Prove knowledge and get your diploma. CHSPE does this, a couple of other states do as well, and this is also the spirit behind the GED program. However, to be clear, the GED does not provide a high school diploma. It does, however, provide something that some employers will accept in lieu of a high school diploma.

There are no, to my knowledge, private programs that offer legitimate high school diplomas in this manner. Should you run a program of this nature and wish to prove me wrong (and I would happily be proven wrong), I urge you to send me an email at tom@thomasnixon.com.

What courses does a typical online program require to earn a diploma?

While this can vary significantly from school to school, a basic program likely requires between 20-22 units to earn a diploma. The break-down can look like this:

Course	# of credits
Math	3
English	4
Science	2
Social Science	4
Fine Arts	1
Foreign Language	2
Health	1
Electives	3
Physical Education	2

Each credit is the equivalent of a one-year course of study. One thing to bear in mind is that this is one example from one school. Other schools will vary somewhat, but should be somewhat similar particularly with the core course (math, science, etc.) requirements. You may see schools where a year-long course is worth ten credits. Adjust accordingly.

Are there additional requirements beyond the diploma-track if I want to go on to college?

A number of schools have two tracks: a diploma-track and a college-track. While both earn you the diploma, the goals are quite different. It is my recommendation that students take the college-track if it is available. You can always change your mind later about attending college, but it will be much more painful if you need to go back and take courses because your college of choice says you require more.

As far as difference in course requirements, typically you will find that those elective courses above magically become additional courses in science and math.

Will I have a teacher?

The simple answer is that typically you will have a teacher. What exactly that looks like can vary dramatically from school. In particular, the exact level of support given by that teacher can be very little or can be quite significant. This is one of the key questions that you should ask any potential school.

Chapter 3: 10 Steps to Online Success

As with anything, doing your due diligence will make you make successful than just charging blindly ahead. It may sound trite, but do your homework!

Step 1: Don't go to school online unless you are prepared to work. This is truly one of the best pieces of advice that I can offer. Often people will go back to school, whether that be college or high school, because they think that they are so supposed to do so. While I strongly encourage potential students to consider going back to school, you really need to be up for it.

Step 2: Determine your age. If you are under a certain age (which could be 18, 19, or 21 typically), you might be able to attend a free online high school. There are a number of public charter schools that allow for students all the way up to age 21. The catch: It will most certainly be in your state and likely your county (or the one next to it). Free can be a really good price!

Step 3: Do your research on potential schools. Yes, price is important, but that is not the most important issue. There are more expensive choices that are better than some less expensive ones, but the reverse is also true.

Step 4: Narrow your list to three schools. There are hundreds of schools. Before you get too far into your search, begin the narrowing process.

Step 5: Interview the school(s). Yes, you interview them. Find out what kind of support that they provide to students. Find out what a classroom looks like. See if they will give you a sample log-in to look at a course.

Step 6: Decide on a school. Yes, eventually you need to choose one school. Since you will notice that a number of these steps involve school selection, this should give you some idea of how important that selection can be.

Step 7: Ask to speak with a teacher. It is amazing what teachers will tell you that others will not.

Step 8: Set a schedule for working on your courses. Yes, online courses are marketed as you being able to work on them whenever you would like, but that is only partially true. You still must get it all done. Determine how many hours a week you should devote to the courses and then do it.

Step 9: Do your homework. I know that this sounds simplistic, but if I had a dime for every online student who told me they fell behind in their assignments because no one was keeping track of it for them, I would be a rather wealthy person.

Step 10: Keep at it. Don't give up. Remember that the hard work is worth the end results. This is exactly what it says. You will need to put time and effort into this or you will fail. Again. That being said, you can do this. Push yourself.

Chapter 4: Accreditation and Diploma Mills

Our students have also told us that online learning works best if you are choosing it. If you are thinking of enrolling only because your parents want you to graduate, try to figure out what excites you about the learning opportunity.

--Minnesota Online High School

Choosing an accredited program provides you with a vital safeguard. While accreditation does not guarantee that it will be an outstanding program, it does provide some assurance of a minimum quality level.

There are two basic forms of accreditation, regional and national. The United States is broken up into six regional accrediting bodies that accredit not only U.S. schools, but some schools abroad as well. In addition to those six regional bodies (see below), there is also a national accreditor of distance learning programs, the Distance Education and Training Council.

In other books and other places, some online high schools are listed that do not have regional or national accreditation. They do, however, have some form of accreditation. At this point, it is unclear how acceptable that alternative accreditation is, but what can be said is that it is not currently accepted by the Council on Higher Education Accreditation and/or by the U.S. Department of Education.

Rather oddly, we have a system of both regional and national accreditation. While both serve their purposes, regional accreditation seems to be more widely accepted. This is less of an issue for high schools than it is for colleges, but you should understand that there are some few colleges that would not accept a DETC diploma. While that number is certainly shrinking, it is still a factor in school selection (and you should check with your schools of choice for guidance).

At present, we live in shifting times with regard to accreditation. CITA, for example, was a collaboration between accreditors to accredit schools which cross regional or national boundaries, but which still operate at the same standard as regionally-accredited schools. CITA accreditation was very much an acceptable form of accreditation.

CITA, though, is now part of AdvancED (www.advanc-ed.org) as is high school components of the Southern Association of Colleges and Schools (SACS CASI), the North Central Association (NCA CASI), and, most recently, the Northwest Accreditation Commission (NWAC).

By the way, you will still see schools listing CITA accreditation. While this is a mistake (because that particular form of accreditation has gone away), it is mostly a harmless one.

There is one other possibility that could be acceptable. Some online high schools have opted to use only state approval. There are states that have such a process and do provide oversight. There are also states that make approval possible, but provide no oversight at all. If a school has state approval and is not listed here, it does not mean it is a poor choice, but rather that the author was not able to determine how the state oversees the approval process.

If you are a state-approved school that is not listed here, please contact the author for possible inclusion in the 2013 edition. Note that acceptable state approval typically comes from Departments of Education.

REGIONAL ACCREDITORS

Below are listed the six regional accreditors. While it is open to debate, it is generally assumed that regional accreditation provides greater flexibility in university choices than does national accreditation.

Although this is difficult to prove, a completely unscientific survey of twenty universities throughout the United States showed that all of the schools would accept students with RA diplomas, but that the number accepting NA diplomas was less. How much less is debatable, but certainly less.

One way to insure that you do not have a problem in that regard is to talk this over with your university of choice prior to selecting your online high school.

Middle States Association of Colleges and Schools (MSA)
Commission on Secondary Schools
3624 Market Street
Philadelphia, PA 19104-2680
Tel: (215) 662-5603
Fax: (215) 662-0957
Web: www.css-msa.org
Email: info@css-msa.org
MSA is the regional accreditor for Delaware, Maryland, New Jersey, New York, Pennsylvania, and the District of Columbia. It also accredits

schools in the Caribbean as well as various locations around the world.

New England Association of Schools and Colleges (NEASC)

Commission on Public Secondary Schools
209 Burlington Rd, Suite 201
Bedford, MA 01730-1433
Tel: (781) 271-0022
Fax: (781) 271-0950
Web: www.neasc.org/cpss/cpss.htm
Email: pgraybennett@neasc.org
NEASC is the regional accreditor for Connecticut, Maine, Massachusetts, New Hampshire, Rhode Island and Vermont and American/international schools in more than sixty nations worldwide.

North Central Association of Colleges and Schools (NCA)

Commission on Accreditation and School Improvement
Arizona State University
PO Box 871008
Tempe, AZ 85287-1008
Tel: (480) 773-6900
Fax: (312) 263-7462
Web: www.ncacasi.org
Email: info@hlcommission.org
NCA is the regional accreditor for Arkansas, Arizona, Colorado, Iowa, Illinois, Indiana, Kansas, Michigan, Minnesota, Missouri, North Dakota, Nebraska, Ohio, Oklahoma, New Mexico, South Dakota, Wisconsin, West Virginia, and Wyoming.

Northwest Accreditation Commission (NWAC)
1910 University Drive
Boise, ID 83725-1060
Tel: (208) 426-5727
Fax: (208) 334-3228
Web: www.boisestate.edu/naas
Email: lpaul@interact.ccsd.net
NWAC is the regional accreditor for Alaska, Idaho, Montana, Nevada, Oregon, Utah, and Washington.

Southern Association of Colleges and Schools (SACS)
Council on Accreditation and School Improvement
1866 Southern Lane
Decatur, GA 30033
Tel: (404) 679-4500
Fax: (404) 679-4541
Web: www.sacscoc.org
Email: melgart@sacscasi.org
SACS is the regional accreditor for Alabama, Florida, Georgia, Kentucky, Louisiana, Mississippi, North Carolina, South Carolina, Tennessee, Texas, and Virginia, and Latin America.

Western Association of Schools and Colleges (WASC)
Accrediting Commission for Schools
533 Airport Boulevard, Suite 200
Burlingame, CA 94010-2009
Tel: (650) 696-1060
Fax: (650) 696-1867
Web: www.acswasc.org
Email: mail@acswasc.org
WASC is the regional accreditor for California, Hawaii, Guam, American Samoa, Commonwealth of the Marianas, the Marshall Islands, the

Federated States of Micronesia, and to American/International Schools in East Asia and the Pacific.

National Accreditors

Since the 2007 version of this book, AdvancEd, as noted above, has become a notable player in accreditation. If a school claims AdvancED accreditation, this is certainly as valid as any of the other accreditors

With more traditional national accreditors, the largest

Distance Education and Training Council (DETC)
1601 18th Street, N.W.
Washington, D.C. 20009
Tel: (202) 234-5100
Fax: (202) 332-1386
Web: www.detc.org
Email: detc@detc.org
DETC is the national accreditor for distance learning programs. There is no requirement that distance learning programs be accredited by DETC and the greater numbers of such programs use solely their regional accreditation. To my knowledge, DETC is not inferior accreditation in the least and, as its sphere of influence grows, acceptability will become less of an issue.

American Academy for Liberal Education
Web: www.aale.org
AALE is relatively new to offering online programs. Within this book, there is only one school that is online (that I was able to find). Look for that to change in the near future as online

programs begin to seek out accreditors that have a solid track record.

DIPLOMA MILLS

With the explosion of the Internet has come an explosion of diploma mills at both the high school and college level. It would be nice if it were possible to say that all online high schools that do not have recognized accreditation are diploma mills. There are several reasons why I do not make this assertion.

First, the author's preference in life is not to be hauled into court. A simple preference, but a real one. Many schools make the choice that they do not wish to be a part of that system. Sometimes the reasoning is related to religious choices and other times because of the cost related to becoming accredited. Making this choice in no way makes them a poor school.

Second, new schools cannot qualify for accreditation. Accreditors want to see that they have an operational history before they can be considered. For example, the Distance Education and Training Council requires that a school be in business a minimum of two years before pursuing accreditation.

Finally, it is not always easy to make the differentiation between a diploma mill and a legally-operating "less than wonderful" school. Is a school operating with state approval, but in a state that provides no oversight on these schools, a legitimate endeavor? Possibly, and that is the concern.

How can you tell if the school you are considering is a diploma mill? While I note that recognized accreditation is one of the components of making that determination, it should be used in conjunction with the other criteria listed below. There are several criteria that can help you in making this determination:

- Does the school have recognized accreditation or state approval?

- Is it possible to determine where the school is located? A website is not an address. The reason why there is no street address is often that these "schools" do not want you to be able to find them after they have your money.

- Does it make outlandish claims? No legal high school diploma can be earned in three days (or seven days or a month). If the website talks about the time to earn it rather than the courses to earn it, be careful.

- Do they have negative listings with the Better Business Bureau? While this is possible even for Harvard University, numerous complaints can be a sure sign of less than ethical behavior. You will want to check with the school's local BBB. This is the other reason why diploma mills do not want to give you a school address.

- Would a diploma from the school be acceptable at the five universities closest to your house? If it is not acceptable at even one of them, it is probably wise to take a pass.

No matter what, it is important to do your research. Make this determination for yourself, but also see what others out there have to say about the school.

Chapter 5: School Listings

Below you will see over 260 online high school listings. It is certain that others exist in the world, so, if you know about these others, please send an email to info@degreepress.com with the relevant information. When the third edition comes out next year, the schools that qualify will be added to the book.

Access Distance Learning
5351 Gordon Persons Building
PO Box 302101
Montgomery, Alabama 36130
United States
Tel: 334.242.9594
Fax: 334.353.5886
Web: accessdl.state.al.us
Email: epatton@alsde.edu
Recognition/Accreditation: Alabama Department of Education
Grade: 1-12
Type: Free, Public
Diploma: Yes
Cost: Free
If free, where?: Alabama
Teen and/or Adult: Teens
Additional information: Access Distance Learning is a program of the State of Alabama and provides opportunities to students in the state who might otherwise not have access to a wide breadth of courses. It provides a greater number of courses for students who attend small, rural schools and other underserved schools. It also offers a number of remediation modules to prepare students for the

Alabama High School Graduation Exam (AHSGE).

Fairbanks B.E.S.T.
BNSBSD Building, 2nd Floor
520 Fifth Avenue
Fairbanks, Alaska 99701
United States
Tel: 877.403.2989
Web: www.fairbanksbest.com
Recognition/Accreditation: Fairbanks North Star Borough District
Grade: 6-12
Type: Charter, Free, Public
Diploma: Yes
Cost: Free
If free, where?: Within the district
Teen and/or Adult: Teens
Additional information: Fairbanks B.E.S.T. utilizes the Advanced Academics curriculum. Parents are the primary managers of the students' education. It has a strong emphasis on community-home support. The B.E.S.T. program allows students to stay involved with the local school for sports. Students also have the ability to take up to two classes at that local school.

North Slope Borough School District
P.O. Box 169
Barrow, Alaska 99723
United States
Tel: 907.852.5311
Web: www.nsbsd.org
Email: david.green@nsbsd.org
Recognition/Accreditation: Alaska Department of Education
Grade: 9-12
Type: Free, Public

Diploma: No
Cost: Free
If free, where?: Within the district
Teen and/or Adult: Teens
Additional information: The school district offers online courses for its students. It is located in Barrow, Alaska. While courses are free, they are only free to students who live within the boundaries of the North Slope Borough School District.

Alberta Distance Learning Centre
4601 - 63 Avenue
(Box 4000)
Barrhead, Alberta T7N 1P4
Canada
Tel: 780.674.5333
Fax: 780.674.7593
Web: www.adlc.ca
Email: information@adlc.ca
Recognition/Accreditation: Provincial Governments
Grade: 1-12
Type: Christian, Free, Public
Diploma: Yes
Cost: Free
If free, where?: Alberta, Northwest Territories, Nunavit provinces
Teen and/or Adult: Teens
Additional information: Alberta Distance Learning Centre offers several programs including a Christian-based one and a French Immersion one. Students may also avail themselves of Work Experience. Program is available to students living in Alberta and to those traveling with their families. Program was founded in 1923. It has grown to include an online learning program as well.

Agave Distance Learning
445 S. Park Avenue
Portable #1
Tucson, Arizona 85719
United States
Tel: 520.225.2677
Web:
www.tusd1.org/contents/distinfo/summer/agave.asp
Email: stuart.baker@tusd1.org
Recognition/Accreditation: Tucson Unified School District
Grade: 9-12
Type: Charter, Free, Public
Diploma: Yes
Cost: Free
If free, where?: Arizona
Teen and/or Adult: Teens
Additional information: While students do not pay for courses offered during the regular school year, there are fees related to summer school courses. Students receive one-to-one instruction with credentialed teachers. Transcripts and diplomas are issued by the Tucson Unified School District. The school offers both Honors and Advanced Placement courses. You have the ability to either earn a diploma or to transfer the credits back to your traditional off-line school.

Arizona Connections Academy
1017 S. Gilbert Road
Suite 209/210
Mesa, Arizona 85204
United States
Tel: 480.782.5842
Fax: 480.782.5845
Web: www.connectionsacademy.com/arizona-

school/home.aspx
Email: info@connectionsacademy.com
Recognition/Accreditation: NCA, Arizona State Board for Charter Schools
Grade: 1-12
Type: Charter, Free, Public
Diploma: Yes
Cost: Free
If free, where?: Arizona
Teen and/or Adult: Teens
Additional information: Arizona Connections Academy is available to students throughout the state and is a tuition-free online charter school. The program meets rigorous state education standards. The school offers services and curricular resources for Special Education students as well.

Arizona Virtual Academy
99 E. Virginia Avenue
Suite 200
Phoenix, Arizona 85004
United States
Tel: 602.476.1320
Fax: 602.595.6874
Web: www.k12.com/azva
Email: azvainfo@azva.org
Recognition/Accreditation: NCA CASI
Grade: 1-12
Type: Charter, Free, Public
Diploma: Yes
Cost: Free
If free, where?: Arizona
Teen and/or Adult: Teens
Additional information: The Arizona Virtual Academy uses the K12.com online curriculum. The program is available to students throughout the state of Arizona. In the elementary years, students

spend less time online than in the later years. This school's program has been successful in meeting the federal government's Adequate Year Progress (AYP) in five of the last six years.

HavasuOnline
2200 Havasupai Blvd
Lake Havasu City, Arizona 86403
United States
Tel: 928.505.6900
Fax: 928.505.6999
Web: havasu.k12.az.us/HavasuOnline/index.htm
Email: info@havasuonline.org
Recognition/Accreditation: Arizona Department of Education, Lake Havasu Unified School District #1
Grade: 7-12
Type: Free, Public
Diploma: Yes
Cost: Free
If free, where?: Lake Havasu City students
Teen and/or Adult: Teens
Additional information: HavasuOnline is a public, tuition-free online school program open to Lake Havasu City students in grades 7–12. Students, depending on their needs, can be either full-time or part-time. This allows for some students to recover credits or to take classes not offered at their traditional high school.

Hope High School Online
5651 W. Talavi Blvd. Ste. 170
Glendale, Arizona 85306
United States
Tel: 800.426.4952
Fax: 602.943.9700
Web: www.hopehighonline.org

Email: hhso@blueprinteducation.org
Recognition/Accreditation: NCA, AdvancED, Arizona State Board of Charter Schools
Grade: 1-12
Type: Charter, Free, Public
Diploma: Yes
Cost: Free
If free, where?: Within the state
Teen and/or Adult: To age 21
Additional information: Hope High School Online offers one of those fairly unique things: a free online school education all the way to age 21. Hope High School Online is supported by the well-known Blueprint Education. HHSO specializes in students whose schedule or special circumstances makes it difficult to attend traditional schools.

Humanities and Sciences Academy
5201 N. 7th Street
Phoenix, Arizona 85014
United States
Tel: 602.650.1333
Fax: 602.650.1777
Web: www.humsci.org
Email: On website
Recognition/Accreditation: DETC
Grade: 9-12
Type: Free
Diploma: Yes
Cost: Free
If free, where?: Within the state
Teen and/or Adult: Teens
Additional information: Humanities and Sciences High School offers a challenging and accelerated program focused on world languages and the core subject areas of English, social studies, mathematics, and natural sciences. Interestingly,

all students are required to take world languages. Unlike other schools that only offer Spanish or French, HumSci offers a wide variety of languages include Danish, Pashto, Swahili, and many more.

Insight School of Arizona
99 E. Virginia Avenue
Suite 200
Phoenix, Arizona 85004
United States
Tel: 866.339.4946
Fax: 602.595.6874
Web: www.k12.com/azva
Email: azvainfo@azva.org
Recognition/Accreditation: NCA CASI
Grade: 7-12
Type: Charter, Free, Public
Diploma: Yes
Cost: Free
If free, where?: Within the state
Teen and/or Adult: Teens
Additional information: Insight Schools are now part of the K12.com group of schools. It offers core courses as well as honors and elective courses. For students who need extra support, it also offers foundation courses. It also offers a dual credit program - high school and college - for students with at least a 2.5 GPA in academic courses.

New World Online Charter
5818 N. 7th Street
Phoenix, Arizona 85014
United States
Tel: 888.399.3087
Web: www.newworldonlinecharter.com
Email: On website
Recognition/Accreditation: Arizona

Department of Education
Grade: 9-12
Type: Charter, Free, Public
Diploma: Yes
Cost: Free
If free, where?: Within the state
Teen and/or Adult: To age 21
Additional information: New World Online Charter uses the curriculum of Advanced Academics. While courses are conducted online, students can get additional tutoring as needed on campus. Laptop computers are also available for checkout. In addition to core courses, NWOC also offers Advanced Placement (AP) courses.

Pinnacle Online High School
2224 W. Southern Avenue
Suite 1
Tempe, Arizona 85282
United States
Tel: 480.755.8222
Fax: 480.755.8223
Web: www.pinnacleeducation.com
Email: enrollment@pin-ed.com
Recognition/Accreditation: NCA
Grade: 9-12
Type: Charter, Free, Public
Diploma: Yes
Cost: Free
If free, where?: Within the state
Teen and/or Adult: Teens
Additional information: Pinnacle Online High School offers online courses to students across Arizona. It was established in 1995. Pinnacle has partnered with Grand Canyon University and students can get credit for dual enrollment. Pinnacle has campuses in Mesa, Tempe (East and

West), Casa Grande, and Nogales.

Primavera Online High School
2471 N. Arizona Avenue
Building 1
Chandler, Arizona 85225
United States
Tel: 480.456.6678
Fax: 480.355.2100
Web: www.primaveratech.org/Online-High-School.aspx
Email: info@primaveratech.org
Recognition/Accreditation: NCA
Grade: 9-12
Type: Charter, Free, Public
Diploma: Yes
Cost: Free
If free, where?: Within the state
Teen and/or Adult: Teens
Additional information: Primavera Online High School is the largest high school in Arizona. The school's students participate in courses in a variety of ways including interactive workbooks, course discussions, and blogs. The school was established in 2001. Primavera courses are aligned to meet state and national standards.

Sequoia Choice High School
1460 South Horne Street
Mesa, Arizona 85204
United States
Tel: 480.461.3222
Fax: 480.649.0747
Web: sequoiachoice.org
Email: info@sequoiachoice.org
Recognition/Accreditation: AdvancED
Grade: 1-12

Type: Charter, Free, Public
Diploma: Yes
Cost: Free
If free, where?: Within the state
Teen and/or Adult: Teens
Additional information: Sequoia Choice Arizona Distance Learning offers a great option for students to earn dual-credit, high school and college credit, for certain courses. The courses are taken at local community colleges and then the credits are transferred into Sequoia. In order to qualify for the program, a student must maintain a 2.5 high school GPA across academic courses.

Arkansas Virtual High School
17 Garren Lane
Enola, Arkansas 72047
United States
Tel: 501.849.3548
Fax: 501.849.2175
Web: arkansashigh.k12.ar.us
Email: avhs@windstream.net
Recognition/Accreditation: Arkansas Department of Education
Grade: 9-12
Type: Free, Public
Diploma: No
Cost: Free
If free, where?: Within the state
Teen and/or Adult: Teens
Additional information: In order to take advantage of the course possibilities with Arkansas Virtual High School, a student must be resident in a district affiliated with the program and be in grades 9 - 12. This is a part-time program, so your local public school district must be affiliated in

order for you to take courses with AVHS.

Coquitlam Open Learning
550 Poirier Street
Coquitlam, British Columbia V3J 6A7
Canada
Tel: 604.936.4285
Fax: 604.936.6594
Web: www.sd43.bc.ca/col
Email: COLAcademicAdvisor@sd43.bc.ca
Recognition/Accreditation: School District #43
Grade: 1-12
Type: Free, Public
Diploma: Yes
Cost: Free
If free, where?: Within the province
Teen and/or Adult: Teens & Adults
Additional information: This school is available only to students in SD43 Secondary School District. It has a number of options including a continual entry program, upgrade courses (to improve grades), and a blended program where students have access to face-to-face teachers.

Antelope Valley Virtual School
California
United States
Tel: 877.557.3916
Web: www.antelopevalleyvirtual.com
Email: On website
Recognition/Accreditation:
Grade: 6-12
Type: Charter, Free, Public
Diploma: Yes
Cost: Free

If free, where?: Surrounding counties
Teen and/or Adult: To age 21
Additional information: Antelope Valley Virtual School utilizes the Advanced Academics curriculum. It serves Kern, Los Angeles, San Bernardino, Ventura, Santa Barbara, San Luis Obispo, Kings, Tulare, and Inyo counties. Antelope Valley Virtual is part of the Abraham Lincoln Independent Study program within Southern Kern Unified School District. It is offered for grades 6-12.

California Virtual Academies

2360 Shasta Way, Unit A
Simi Valley, California 93065
United States
Tel: 866.339.6787
Fax: 805.581.0330
Web: www.k12.com/cava/
Email: info@caliva.org
Recognition/Accreditation: WASC
Grade: 1-12
Type: Charter, Free, Public
Diploma: Yes
Cost: Free
If free, where?: California
Teen and/or Adult: Teens
Additional information: California Virtual Academies utilizes the K12.com curriculum. It is free to students across California. Key components, in addition to a strong academic foundation, is the building of an appreciation for diversity and the development of an awareness of the importance of cultural sensitivity. CAVA is a chain of schools with locations in Jamestown, Kern, Kings, Los Angeles, San Diego, San Joaquin, San Mateo, Santa Ysabel, Sonoma, and Sutter counties.

Capistrano Connections Academy

26800 Aliso Viejo Parkway
Suite 120
Aliso Viejo, California 92656
United States
Tel: 949.461.1667
Fax: 949.425.8791
Web: www.connectionsacademy.com/california-southern-capistrano-school/home.aspx
Email: jhorowitz@connectionsacademy.com
Recognition/Accreditation: WASC, AdvancEd
Grade: 1-12
Type: Charter, Free, Public
Diploma: Yes
Cost: Free
If free, where?: Surrounding counties
Teen and/or Adult: Teens
Additional information: Connections Academies are part of a chain of online schools. Personalized learning is a key component of Connections Academy. Typically, these academies are charter schools and are free to students residing in specific counties. This Connections Academy operates in the counties of Los Angeles, San Diego, Orange, Riverside, and San Bernardino.

Central California Connections Academy

4020 S. Demaree St., Suite B
Visalia, California 93277
United States
Tel: 800.382.6010 / 559.713.1324
Fax: 559.713.1330
Web: www.connectionsacademy.com/california-central-school/home.aspx
Email: info@connectionseducation.com
Recognition/Accreditation: WASC
Grade: 1-12

Type: Charter, Free, Public
Diploma: Yes
Cost: Free
If free, where?: Surrounding counties
Teen and/or Adult: Teens
Additional information: Connections Academies are part of a chain of online schools. Personalized learning is a key component of Connections Academy. Typically, these academies are charter schools and are free to students residing in specific counties. This particular Connections Academy operates within the counties of Fresno, Inyo, Kern, Kings, and Tulare.

Choice 2000 Online High School
755 North A Street
Perris, California 92570
United States
Tel: 951.940.5700
Fax: 951.940.5706
Web: www.choice2000.org
Email: latricia.parker@puhsd.org
Recognition/Accreditation: WASC
Grade: 9-12
Type: Charter, Free, Public
Diploma: Yes
Cost: Free
If free, where?: Surrounding counties
Teen and/or Adult: Teens
Additional information: Choice 2000 is the first public high school to be both fully online and WASC accredited. Choice 2000 serves students in the counties of Riverside, San Bernardino, Orange, San Diego, and Imperial. Classes are held in real-time, so the structure is closer to a traditional school day. Students have the option of the following educational tracks: Traditional, Credit

Recovery, Community College Concurrent Enrollment, and Early Graduation.

Clovis Online School

1655 David E. Cook Way
Clovis, California 93611
United States
Tel: 559.327.4400
Fax: 559.327.4490
Web: onlineschool.cusd.com
Email: On Website
Recognition/Accreditation: WASC
Grade: 9-12
Type: Charter, Free, Public
Diploma: Yes
Cost: Free
If free, where?: Surrounding counties
Teen and/or Adult: To age 21
Additional information: Clovis Online School is part of the Clovis Unified School District. It serves the students of Fresno, Madera, Merced, Mono, Inyo, Tulare, Kings, San Benito, and Monterey counties. Clovis Online School allows for flexibility in the time necessary to complete assignments.

Delta Pacific Online

Tracy, California
United States
Tel: 877.705.4612
Web: www.deltapacificonline.com
Email: On website
Recognition/Accreditation: WASC
Grade: 6-12
Type: Charter, Free, Public
Diploma: Yes
Cost: Free

If free, where?: Surrounding counties
Teen and/or Adult: Teens
Additional information: Delta Pacific Online utilizes the curriculum of Advanced Academics. Delta Pacific Online is part of Delta Charter School. It operates in a number of counties including San Joaquin, Contra Costa, Alameda, Santa Clara, Stanislaus, Calaveras, Amador, and Sacramento.

Dunlap Leadership Academy
NorCal Online School Network
California
United States
Tel: 877.744.5216
Web: dunlapleadershipacademy.com
Email: On website
Recognition/Accreditation: Kings Canyon Unified School District
Grade: 9-12
Type: Charter, Free, Public
Diploma: Yes
Cost: Free
If free, where?: Surrounding counties
Teen and/or Adult: To age 21
Additional information: Courses are open to residents of the Kings Canyon Unified School District in Fresno County and the surrounding counties. The school uses curriculum from Advanced Academics. Up-to-date progress reports are regularly available to students and parents.

Elk Grove Unified School District Virtual Academy
5900 Bamford Drive
Sacramento, California 95823
United States
Tel: 916.686.7747

Web: www.k12local.com/elkgrove
Email: egvirtual@egusd.net
Recognition/Accreditation: Elk Grove Unified School District
Grade: 1-12
Type: Charter, Free, Public
Diploma: Yes
Cost: Free
If free, where?: Sacramento and surrounding counties
Teen and/or Adult: Teens
Additional information: Elk Grove Unified School District t Virtual Academy offers an online program to students in Sacramento, Amador, Yolo, El Dorado, Placer, Contra Costa, Solano, Sutter, and San Joaquin counties. It utilizes the K12.com curriculum.

Golden State Virtual Academy
800 West Elm Street
Bishop, California 93514
United States
Tel: 877.594.4863
Web: goldenstateva.com/Online-High-School.aspx
Email: On website
Recognition/Accreditation:
Grade: 9-12
Type: Charter, Free, Public
Diploma: Yes
Cost: Free
If free, where?: Surrounding counties
Teen and/or Adult: To age 21
Additional information: Golden State Virtual Academy serves students in Fresno, Inyo, Kern, Mono, San Bernardino, and Tulare Counties. Former name: Mt. Whitney Virtual Academy.

Currently seeking accreditation through WASC.

Golden Valley Virtual Charter School
2421 Portola Road
Suite C
Ventura, California 93003
United States
Tel: 877.347.2612
Fax: 805.642.3468
Web: www.goldenvalleyvirtual.com
Email: gvcsterri@sbcglobal.net
Recognition/Accreditation: WASC
Grade: 6-12
Type: Charter, Free, Public
Diploma: Yes
Cost: Free
If free, where?: Kern, Ventura, Santa Barbara, Los Angeles Counties
Teen and/or Adult: To age 21
Additional information: Golden Valley Virtual Charter School uses curriculum from Advanced Academics. Students must complete work every school day or they will be marked absent. The school allows concurrent enroll at community colleges and will accept the courses for transfer credit. The program operates in Kern, Ventura, Santa Barbara, and Los Angeles counties.

iHigh Virtual Academy
2375 Congress Street
San Diego, California 92110
United States
Tel: 619.209.4593
Fax: 619.209.4566
Web: www.sandi.net/ihigh
Email: pmacintyre@sandi.net
Recognition/Accreditation: WASC

Grade: 9-12
Type: Free, Public
Diploma: Yes
Cost: Free
If free, where?: Within the district
Teen and/or Adult: Teens
Additional information: iHigh Virtual Academy is part of the San Diego Unified School District. Students have weekly deadlines and assignments that need to be completed. While the format is flexible, the school makes it clear that the curriculum is rigorous and suitable for college-bound students. The importance of being self-directed is a cornerstone of the school. The content teacher proctors exams and student labs. Laptop computers are available for check-out.

Insight School of California - Los Angeles
1202 West Avenue J
Suite 100
Lancaster, California   93534
United States
Tel: 800.670.5391
Fax: 661.945.6657
Web: cala.insightschools.net
Email: info@insightca.net
Recognition/Accreditation: NWAC, WASC
Grade: 9-12
Type: Charter, Free, Public
Diploma: Yes
Cost: Free
If free, where?: Within the county
Teen and/or Adult: Teens
Additional information: Insight Schools are now part of the K12.com group of schools. It offers core courses as well as honors and elective courses. For students who need extra support, it also offers

foundation courses. It also offers a dual credit program - high school and college - for students with   at   least   a   2.5   GPA.

Insight School of California - North Bay
8733 Lakewood Drive
Suite B
Windsor, California 95492
United States
Tel: 800.670.5391
Fax: 866.653.1007
Web: canb.insightschools.net
Email: info@insightcanb.net
Recognition/Accreditation: NWAC, WASC
Grade: 9-12
Type: Charter, Free, Public
Diploma: Yes
Cost: Free
If free, where?: Within the county
Teen and/or Adult: Teens
Additional information: Insight Schools are now part of the K12.com group of schools. It offers core courses as well as honors and elective courses. For students who need extra support, it also offers foundation courses. It also offers a dual credit program - high school and college - for students with at least a 2.5 GPA in academic courses.

iQ Academy California: Los Angeles
1830 Nogales Street
Rowland Heights, California 91748
United States
Tel: 888.997.4722
Fax: 888.260.5368
Web: losangeles.iqacademyca.com
Email: info@losangeles.iQacademyCA.com
Recognition/Accreditation: Rowland Unified

School District
Grade: 1-12
Type: Charter, Free, Public
Diploma: Yes
Cost: Free
If free, where?: Los Angeles, Kern, Orange, San Bernardino, Ventura Counties
Teen and/or Adult: To age 21
Additional information: iQ Academy is now part of the K12.com chain of schools. While iQ was once solely a high school program, this change has allowed it the opportunity to offer a program for grades Kindergarten to 12th grade. The Academy is available for free to students living within the counties of Los Angeles, Kern, Orange, San Bernardino, and Ventura counties.

Juan Bautista de Anza Online Charter School

583 Palm Canyon Drive, Suite A
Borrego Springs, California 92004
United States
Tel: 760.767.5850
Web: jbdaonlinecharterschool.net
Email: jbdacharterschool@att.net
Recognition/Accreditation: WASC
Grade: 6-12
Type: Charter, Free, Public
Diploma: Yes
Cost: Free
If free, where?: San Diego and surrounding counties
Teen and/or Adult: Teens
Additional information: Juan Bautista de Anza Charter School uses curriculum from Advanced Academics. The school offers Advanced Placement courses. It also offers a unique program in Horse

Wisdom and provides a special emphasis on service learning projects.

National University Academy
2030 University Drive
Vista, California 92083
United States
Tel: 877.252.7786
Web: ahs.nusystem.org
Recognition/Accreditation: WASC
Grade: 6-12
Type: Charter, Free, Public
Diploma: Yes
Cost: Free
If free, where?: Surrounding counties
Teen and/or Adult: Teens
Additional information: National University Academy is part of the National University System of schools. This is its public charter school version of its online high school. Unlike its sister school, National University Virtual High School, this program is free to students who live in certain locations. NUA consists of four charter schools in San Diego, Fresno County, Tulare County, and Armona. There is some required seat time. The Armona campus provides courses for the California Conservation Corps or Workforce in Action.

Pivot Online Charter School, North Bay
California
United States
Tel: 877.544.1428
Web: www.pivotnorthbay.com
Email: On website
Recognition/Accreditation: Roads Education Organization / California Department of Education

Grade: 6-12
Type: Charter, Free, Public
Diploma: Yes
Cost: Free
If free, where?: Surrounding counties
Teen and/or Adult: To age 21
Additional information: Pivot Charter School, North Bay, uses curriculum from Advanced Academics. Full-time enrollment is required. Courses must be completed during the traditional semester schedule. Students will still be required to participate in mandated state testing. This includes STAR and CAHSEE. You would need to come to a testing location. Serves students in Sonoma, Solano, Mendocino, Lake, Napa, and Marin Counties.

Pivot Online Charter School, North Valley
California
United States
Tel: 877.544.1423
Web: www.pivotnorthvalley.com
Email: On website
Recognition/Accreditation: Roads Education Organization / California Department of Education
Grade: 6-12
Type: Charter, Free, Public
Diploma: Yes
Cost: Free
If free, where?: Surrounding counties
Teen and/or Adult: To age 21
Additional information: Pivot Charter School, North Valley, uses curriculum from Advanced Academics. Full-time enrollment is required. Courses must be completed during the traditional semester schedule. Students will still be required to

participate in mandated state testing. This includes STAR and CAHSEE. You would need to come to a testing location. Serves students in Butte, Tehama, Plumas, Yuba, Sutter, Colusa, and Glenn counties.

Pivot Online Charter School, Riverside
Riverside, California
United States
Tel: 888.704.5498
Web: www.pivotriverside.com
Email: On website
Recognition/Accreditation: Roads Education Organization / California Department of Education
Grade: 6-12
Type: Charter, Free, Public
Diploma: Yes
Cost: Free
If free, where?: Surrounding counties
Teen and/or Adult: To age 21
Additional information: Pivot Charter School, Riverside, uses curriculum from Advanced Academics. Full-time enrollment is required. Courses must be completed during the traditional semester schedule. Students will still be required to participate in mandated state testing. This includes STAR and CAHSEE. You would need to come to a testing location. Serves students in Riverside, Orange, San Diego, Imperial, and San Bernardino counties.

Pivot Online Charter School, San Diego
San Diego, California
United States
Tel: 877.544.1429
Web: www.advancedacademics.com/pivot-san-diego-charter-school/index.html

Email: On website
Recognition/Accreditation: WASC
Grade: 6-12
Type: Charter, Free, Public
Diploma: Yes
Cost: Free
If free, where?: Surrounding counties
Teen and/or Adult: To age 21
Additional information: Pivot Charter School, San Diego, uses curriculum from Advanced Academics. Full-time enrollment is required. Courses must be completed during the traditional semester schedule. Students will still be required to participate in mandated state testing. This includes STAR and CAHSEE. You would need to come to a testing location. Students can come from the counties of San Diego, Orange, Riverside, and Imperial.

Riverside Virtual School
6401 Lincoln Avenue
Riverside, California 92506
United States
Tel: 951.276.2006
Fax: 951.778.5623
Web: rusdtech.net
Email: dhaglund@rusd.k12.ca.us
Recognition/Accreditation: WASC
Grade: 6-12
Type: Charter, Free, Public
Diploma: No
Cost: Free
If free, where?: Surrounding counties
Teen and/or Adult: Teens
Additional information: Riverside Virtual School serves students in Riverside, Imperial, Orange, San Diego, and San Bernardino counties. It

is an approved provider of online courses for A-G purposes with the UC/CSU systems. Riverside Virtual School also partners with other school districts throughout the state to provide courses.

San Diego Virtual School
496 Third Avenue
Chula Vista, California 91910
United States
Tel: 888.704.5498
Web: www.sdvirtualschools.com
Recognition/Accreditation: California Department of Education
Grade: 6-12
Type: Charter, Free, Public
Diploma: Yes
Cost: Free
If free, where?: Surrounding counties
Teen and/or Adult: To age 21
Additional information: San Diego Virtual School utilizes the Advanced Academics curriculum. It serves the students of San Diego, Orange, Riverside, and Imperial counties. The school offers a variety of field trips and clubs.

San Francisco Flex Academy
555 Post Street
San Francisco, California 94102
United States
Tel: 877.382.0242
Fax: 415.674.7748
Web: www.k12.com/sfflex
Email: info@flexsf.org
Recognition/Accreditation: WASC
Grade: 9-12
Type: Charter, Free, Public
Diploma: Yes

Cost: Free
If free, where?: Within the state
Teen and/or Adult: Teens
Additional information: San Francisco Flex Academy is a blended learning school. It uses online curriculum, but students are required to attend the school on-site five days a week.

Silicon Valley Flex Academy
610 Jarvis Drive
Morgan Hill, California 95037
United States
Tel: 877.382.3466
Fax: 408.778.7591
Web: www.k12.com/svflex
Email: info@svflex.org
Recognition/Accreditation: WASC
Grade: 6-12
Type: Charter, Free, Public
Diploma: Yes
Cost: Free
If free, where?: Within the state
Teen and/or Adult: Teens
Additional information: Silicon Valley Flex Academy is a blended learning school. It uses online curriculum, but students are required to attend the school on-site five days a week.

UC Online Academy
UCSC Extension Silicon Valley
2505 Augustine Drive, Suite 100
Santa Clara, California 95054
United States
Tel: 408.450.4938
Web: ucoa.org
Email: kheller@ucoa.org
Recognition/Accreditation: University of

California
Grade: 9-12
Type: Free, Public
Diploma: No
Cost: Free
If free, where?: Within the state
Teen and/or Adult: Teens
Additional information: UC Online Academy is part of the prestigious University of California system. Courses will be available beginning in the fall of 2012. UCOA offers courses primarily to provide students with the opportunity to take courses not offered at their home school in order to gain admittance into a campus of the University of California. The school offers a wide breadth of Advanced Placement, Honors, and a - g courses.

University of California College Prep
California
United States
Web: www.uccp.org
Recognition/Accreditation:
Grade: 9-12
Type: Free, Public
Diploma: No
Cost: Free
If free, where?: Within the district
Teen and/or Adult: Teens
Additional information: Offers online courses free to school districts and to individuals. For assessment, students would need to take the course through one of UCCP's partner districts. While it used to offer online courses as a provider, it now gives away the content. It is not open for enrollment.

Academy Online High School

Academy School District 20
1110 Chapel Hills Drive
Colorado Springs, Colorado 80920
United States
Tel: 719.234.1670
Fax: 719.234.1732
Web: www.asd20.org/aohs
Email: helpdesk@d20onlineschool.org
Recognition/Accreditation: Colorado State
Department of Education
Grade: 9-12
Type: Free, Public
Diploma: Yes
Cost: Free
If free, where?: Within the district
Teen and/or Adult: Teens
Additional information: Academy Online High students can earn dual credits with Colorado Technical University. The dual credit courses can lead to an Association of Science in Information Systems or an Associate of Science in Business.

Branson School Online

101 Saddle Rock Drive
PO Box 128
Branson, Colorado 81027
United States
Tel: 888.863.7850
Fax: 866.387.7834
Web: www.bransonschoolonline.com
Email: info@bransonschoolonline.com
Recognition/Accreditation: Colorado
Department of Education
Grade: 1-12
Type: Free, Public
Diploma: Yes

Cost: Free
If free, where?: Colorado
Teen and/or Adult: Teens
Additional information: Branson School Online (BSO) is funded through the Colorado Department of Education. It was founded in 2001 and is a public online school. It focuses on offering a high-quality curriculum presented by teachers licensed in the State of Colorado.

Colorado Connections Academy
8 Inverness Drive East
Englewood, Colorado 80112
United States
Tel: 303.794.2302
Fax: 303.794.2179
Web: www.connectionsacademy.com/colorado-school/home.aspx
Email: info@connectionsacademy.com
Recognition/Accreditation: NCA CASI
Grade: 1-12
Type: Charter, Free, Public
Diploma: Yes
Cost: Free
If free, where?: Colorado
Teen and/or Adult: Teens
Additional information: Connections Academies are part of a chain of well-known online schools. Personalized learning is a key component of Connections Academy. Typically, these academies are charter schools and are free to students residing in Colorado. This program is offered by Mapleton Public Schools.

Colorado Distance and Electronic Learning Academy (CDELA)
4700 E. Bromley Lane, Ste. 205

Brighton, Colorado 80601
United States
Tel: 866.442.3352
Fax: 303.637.9273
Web: www.cdela.com
Email: cdela.info@cdela.com
Recognition/Accreditation: Colorado Charter School Institute
Grade: 1-12
Type: Charter, Free, Public
Diploma: Yes
Cost: Free
If free, where?: Colorado
Teen and/or Adult: Teens
Additional information: CDELA provides use of a complete computer system including technical support and reimbursement for Internet charges. All teachers are licensed by the State of Colorado.

Colorado Virtual Academy
11990 Grant Street
Suite 402
Northglenn, Colorado 80233
United States
Tel: 866.339.6814
Fax: 303.255.7044
Web: www.k12.com/cova
Email: info@covcs.org
Recognition/Accreditation: Adams 12 Five Start School District
Grade: 1-12
Type: Charter, Free, Public
Diploma: Yes
Cost: Free
If free, where?: Colorado
Teen and/or Adult: Teens

Additional information: Colorado Virtual Academy uses K12.com curriculum. Students can earn a diploma through Colorado Virtual Academy and Adams 12 Five Star school district based upon successful completion and mastery of course content.

Denver Online High School
1350 East 33rd Avenue
Denver, Colorado 80205
United States
Tel: 720.424.8281
Fax: 720.424.8279
Web: online.dpsk12.org
Email: Online_High@dpsk12.org
Recognition/Accreditation: Colorado Department of Education
Grade: 9-12
Type: Free, Public
Diploma: Yes
Cost: Free
If free, where?: Within the state
Teen and/or Adult: Teens
Additional information: Denver Online High School uses Odysseyware curriculum. It is a part of the Denver Public Schools. In addition to the core curriculum, students have access to Advanced Placement courses as well as tuition-free college courses.

eDCSD / Colorado Cyber
312 Cantril Street
Room 115
Castle Rock, Colorado 80104
United States
Tel: 303.387.9465
Web: edcsd.org

Email: edcsd@dcsdk12.org
Recognition/Accreditation: Douglas County School District
Grade: 1-12
Type: Free, Public
Diploma: Yes
Cost: Free
If free, where?: Colorado
Teen and/or Adult: Teens
Additional information: Colorado Cyber is an online school that is available throughout the state of Colorado. It is offered by Douglas County School District. Colorado Cyber uses curriculum from Lincoln Interactive. The school offers field trips, school events, and its own social network. Colorado Cyber combines face-to-face and online learning.

HOPE Online Learning Academy Co-op
367 Inverness Parkway
Suite 225
Englewood, Colorado 80112
United States
Tel: 303.989.3539
Fax: 303.675.3013
Web: hopeco-op.org
Email: info@hopeonline.org
Recognition/Accreditation: Douglas County School District
Grade: 1-12
Type: Charter, Free, Public
Diploma: Yes
Cost: Free
If free, where?: Within the state
Teen and/or Adult: Teens
Additional information: Hope Online has a focus on individualized instruction. It is the only public school in Colorado that provides students

with online learning and that includes individualized learning plans. Students also receive in-person support to improve student success rates.

Insight School of Colorado
8601 Turnpike Drive
Suite 210
Westminster, Colorado 80031
United States
Tel: 800.705.1528
Fax: 303.728.6266
Web: co.insightschools.net
Email: info@insightcohs.net
Recognition/Accreditation: NWAC
Grade: 9-12
Type: Charter, Free, Public
Diploma: Yes
Cost: Free
If free, where?: Within the state
Teen and/or Adult: Teens
Additional information: Insight Schools are now part of the K12.com group of schools. It offers core courses as well as honors and elective courses. For students who need extra support, it also offers foundation courses. It also offers a dual credit program - high school and college - for students with at least a 2.5 GPA in academic courses.

JeffCo's 21st Century Virtual Academy
1829 Denver West Drive, #27
Golden, Colorado 80401
United States
Tel: 303.982.6770
Fax: 303.982.6774
Web: jeffcopublicschools.org/online/index.html
Email: learnonline@jeffco.k12.co.us
Recognition/Accreditation: Jeffco Public

Schools
Grade: 7-12
Type: Public
Diploma: Yes
Cost: Free
If free, where?: Colorado
Teen and/or Adult: To age 21
Additional information: While it is clearly part of Jefferson County Public Schools, one need not live in the district or the county to register for courses. However, you must be under 21 and reside in the state of Colorado. One of its teachers was named 2011 Online Teacher of the Year by Southern Regional Education Board (SREB) and the International Association for K-12 Online Learning (iNACOL).

Karval Online Education
Karval School District RE-23 16232 County Road 29
Karval, Colorado 80823
United States
Tel: 719.446.5313
Fax: 719.446.5331
Web: online.karvalschool.org
Recognition/Accreditation: Colorado Department of Education
Grade: 1-12
Type: Free, Public
Diploma: Yes
Cost: Free
If free, where?: Colorado
Teen and/or Adult: Teens
Additional information: Local Karval students may participate in extracurricular activities at Karval High School. Non-local students can participate in their district of residence. Junior and

seniors may take courses through local community colleges. Students in grades 7 - 9 can apply for the CollegeInvest Early Achievers Scholarship.

Monte Vista On-Line Academy
345 East Prospect Ave
Monte Vista, Colorado 81144
United States
Tel: 719.852.2212
Fax: 719.852.6184
Web: www.monte.k12.co.us/ola/index.htm
Email: dirk@monte.k12.co.us
Recognition/Accreditation: Colorado Department of Education, NCAA
Grade: 6-12
Type: Free, Public
Diploma: Yes
Cost: Free
If free, where?: Within the state
Teen and/or Adult: Teens
Additional information: OLA is part of the Monte Vista School District. It is the oldest online school in Colorado having been founded in 1997. OLA also offers an online GED program.

Provost Academy Colorado
7730 E. Belleview Avenue
Suite AG-9
Greenwood Village, Colorado 80111
United States
Tel: 888.472.2656 / 303.770.1240
Web: co.provostacademy.com
Email: info@provostacademy.ocom
Recognition/Accreditation: Colorado Department of Education
Grade: 9-12
Type: Charter, Free, Public

Diploma: Yes
Cost: Free
If free, where?: Colorado
Teen and/or Adult: To age 21
Additional information: Provost Academy Colorado is a STEM-Focused (Science, Technology, Engineering, Math) online high school. Provost Academy is owned by EdisonLearning. Each student has their own individualized learning plan.

CT Virtual Learning
85 Alumni Rd.
Newington, Connecticut 06111
United States
Tel: 860.832.3891
Fax: 860.666.3891
Web: www.ctvirtuallearning.com
Email: ghayden@ctdlc.org
Recognition/Accreditation: Connecticut Department of Education
Grade: 9-12
Type: Free, Public
Diploma: No
Cost: $199 - $699 (or free; see below.)
Teen and/or Adult: Teens
Additional information: Courses through CT Virtual Learning may be free. While CT Virtual Learning does charge the local school, it is up to that same local school to decide whether or not it will charge the student. CT Virtual Learning is a state-wide online learning effort.

Broward Virtual School
6600 SW Nova Drive
Davie, Florida 33317
United States
Tel: 754.321.110

Fax: 754.321.1115
Web: www.bved.net
Email: On website
Recognition/Accreditation: SACS
Grade: 1-12
Type: Free, Public
Diploma: Yes
Cost: Free
If free, where?: Within the county
Teen and/or Adult: Teens
Additional information: Broward Virtual School partners with Florida Virtual School for middle and high school curriculum. BVS was the top performing Florida Virtual School franchise in Florida for school years 2008-09 and 2009-10. BVS uses K12, Inc. for its elementary school program.

Calhoun Virtual Instruction Program
20859 Central Avenue E
RM-G20
Blountstown, Florida 32424
United States
Tel: 866.339.8784
Web: www.k12local.com/calhoun
Email: On website
Recognition/Accreditation: On website
Grade: 6-12
Type: Charter, Free, Public
Diploma: Yes
Cost: Free
If free, where?: Within the county
Teen and/or Adult: Teens
Additional information: Available to students who reside within the borders of Calhoun County.

Citrus Virtual Instruction Program
400 Lake Mary Blvd

Sanford, Florida 32773
United States
Tel: 866.339.8784
Web: www.k12local.com/citrus
Recognition/Accreditation:
Grade: 5-12
Type: Charter, Free, Public
Diploma: Yes
Cost: Free
If free, where?: Within the county
Teen and/or Adult: Teens
Additional information: Available to students who reside within the borders of Citrus County.

Clay Virtual Academy
23 South Green Street
Green Cove Springs, Florida 32043
United States
Tel: 866.339.8784
Web: www.k12local.com/clay
Grade: 6-12
Type: Charter, Free, Public
Diploma: Yes
Cost: Free
If free, where?: Within the county
Teen and/or Adult: Teens
Additional information: Available to students who reside within the borders of Clay County.

Florida Virtual Academies
Florida
Tel: 855.748.4737
Web: www.k12.com/flva
Recognition/Accreditation: On website
Grade: 1-12
Type: Charter, Free, Public
Diploma: Yes

Cost: Free
If free, where?: Within the state
Teen and/or Adult: Teens
Additional information: Florida Virtual Academies utilize the K12, Inc. curriculum.

Florida Virtual Program
1909 N. 3rd Street
Jacksonville Beach, Florida 32250
United States
Tel: 904.247.3268
Fax: 904.247.3276
Web: www.K12.com/flvp
Email: lfuhrmeister@K12.com
Recognition/Accreditation: Sheboygan Area School District Charter Schools
Grade: 1-12
Type: Free, Public
Diploma: Yes
Cost: Free
If free, where?: Florida
Teen and/or Adult: Teens
Additional information: The Florida Virtual Program is a group of virtual district programs that is managed by K12 Inc. It has consistently earned a grade of 'A' on the Florida Department of Education's report card. In addition to its core program, it also offers an advanced learner program for students who need a greater challenge.

Florida Virtual School
2145 Metrocenter Blvd
Suite 200
Orlando, Florida 32835
United States
Tel: 407.513.3587
Fax: 407.513.3480

Web: www.flvs.net
Email: info@flvs.net
Recognition/Accreditation: SACS, NCAA
Grade: 1-12
Type: Free, Public
Diploma: Yes
Cost: Free
If free, where?: Florida
Teen and/or Adult: Teens
Additional information: Florida Virtual School is the largest online school in the United States. Students can either complete the full-time program with FLVS or they can transfer individual courses back to their school districts. Beginning with the 2012-2013 school year, Florida Virtual School is now able to offer a diploma for full-time students.

Glades Virtual Instruction Program
400 10th Street SW
Moore Haven, Florida 33471
United States
Tel: 866.339.8784
Web: www.k12local.com/glades
Recognition/Accreditation:
Grade: 6-12
Type: Charter, Free, Public
Diploma: Yes
Cost: Free
If free, where?: Within the county
Teen and/or Adult: Teens
Additional information: Available to students who reside within the boundaries of Glades County.

Hillsborough County Online Instruction Program
129 E. 124th Avenue
Tampa, Florida 33612

United States
Tel: 813.983.7278
Web: www.k12local.com/hillsborough
Recognition/Accreditation:
Grade: 6-12
Type: Charter, Free, Public
Diploma: Yes
Cost: Free
If free, where?: Within the county
Teen and/or Adult: Teens
Additional information: Available to students who reside in Hillsborough County.

Miami Dade Online Academy
150 NE 2nd Avenue
Miami, Florida 33132
United States
Tel: 866.339.8784
Web: www.k12local.com/miamidade
Recognition/Accreditation:
Grade: 5-12
Type: Charter, Free, Public
Diploma: Yes
Cost: Free
If free, where?: Within the county
Teen and/or Adult: Teens
Additional information: Available to students who reside in Miami-Dade County. Miami Dade Online Academy utilizes the K12, Inc. curriculum.

Miami-Dade Virtual School
1450 NE Second Avenue
Miami, Florida 33132
United States
Tel: 305.995.1000
Web: mdvs.dadeschools.net
Email: On website

Recognition/Accreditation: Miami-Dade County Public Schools
Grade: 9-12
Type: Public
Diploma: No
Cost: Free
If free, where?: Within the district
Teen and/or Adult: Teens
Additional information: Miami-Dade Virtual School (M-DVS) provides online options for students to earn high school credits. This school offers thirteen online courses in the areas of language arts, science, foreign language, math, social studies, health, and physical education. M-DVS uses the Florida Virtual School curriculum.

Orange County Virtual School
445 West Amelia Street
ELC 8th Floor
Orlando, Florida 32801
United States
Tel: 866.339.8784
Web: www.k12local.com/orange
Recognition/Accreditation:
Grade: 5-12
Type: Charter, Free, Public
Diploma: Yes
Cost: Free
If free, where?: Within the county
Teen and/or Adult: Teens
Additional information: Available to students who reside within Orange County.

Pivot Charter School, Florida (Fort Myers)
2675 Winkler Avenue
Suite 200
Fort Myers, Florida 33901

United States
Tel: 877.410.1054 / 239.243.8266
Web: www.pivotcharterschool.com
Recognition/Accreditation: Florida
Department of Education
Grade: 6-12
Type: Charter, Free, Public
Diploma: Yes
Cost: Free
If free, where?: Within the county
Teen and/or Adult: Teens
Additional information: Students must live in Lee County, Florida to attend the Fort Myers School and must live in Hillsborough, Florida to attend the Tampa school. Pivot Charter School utilizes the Advanced Academics curriculum.

Pivot Charter School, Florida (Tampa)
3020 South Falkenburg Road
Riverview, Florida 33569
United States
Tel: 877.410.1054 / 813.626.6724
Web: pivotcharterschool.com
Recognition/Accreditation: Florida
Department of Education
Grade: 6-12
Type: Charter, Free, Public
Diploma: Yes
Cost: Free
If free, where?: Within the county
Teen and/or Adult: To age 21
Additional information: Students must live in Lee County, Florida to attend the Fort Myers School and must live in Hillsborough, Florida to attend the Tampa school. Pivot Charter School utilizes the digital curriculum from Advanced Academics.

Sarasota Virtual School
1960 Landings Blvd
Blue First Floor
Sarasota, Florida 34231
United States
Tel: 866.339.8784
Web: www.k12local.com/sarasota
Recognition/Accreditation:
Grade: 5-12
Type: Charter, Free, Public
Diploma: Yes
Cost: Free
If free, where?: Within the county
Teen and/or Adult: Teens
Additional information: Available to students who reside in Sarasota County.

Volusia Virtual School
1250 Reed Canal Road
Port Orange, Florida 32129
United States
Tel: 386.255.6475 x38342
Web: www.k12local.com/volusia
Recognition/Accreditation:
Grade: 6-12
Type: Charter, Free, Public
Diploma: Yes
Cost: Free
If free, where?: Within the county
Teen and/or Adult: Teens
Additional information: Available to students who reside within Volusia County.

Georgia Cyber Academy
503 Oak Place
Suite 540
Atlanta, Georgia 30349

United States
Tel: 404.684.8824
Fax: 404.684.8816
Web: www.K12.com/gca/
Recognition/Accreditation: AdvancED, SACS
Grade: 1-12
Type: Charter, Free, Public
Diploma: Yes
Cost: Free
Teen and/or Adult: Teens
Additional information: Georgia Cyber Academy is an online charter school that utilizes the K12 digital curriculum. The school includes an Advanced Learner program for selected students.

Hawaii Technology Academy
94-810 Moloalo Street
2nd Floor
Waipahu, Hawaii 96797
United States
Tel: 808.676.5444
Fax: 808.676.5470
Web: www.K12.com/hta/
Email: rleonardi@hawaiitechacademy.org
Recognition/Accreditation: WASC
Grade: 1-12
Type: Charter, Free, Public
Diploma: Yes
Cost: Free
If free, where?: Within the state
Teen and/or Adult: Teens
Additional information: Hawaii Technology Academy is available to students who reside on the islands of Oahu, Kauai, Maui, Lanai, Molokai, and the Big Island. The school utilizes curriculum from K12 and offers an Advanced Learning program.

Idaho Connects Online School

12639 W. Explorer Drive, Suite 185
Boise, Idaho 83713
United States
Tel: 208.287.3668
Fax: 208.287.3671
Web: idahoconnectsonline.org/
Email: enrollment@iconschool.org
Recognition/Accreditation: AdvancED
Grade: 6-12
Type: Charter, Free, Public
Diploma: Yes
Cost: Free
If free, where?: Idaho
Teen and/or Adult: Teens
Additional information: This school was formerly Kaplan Academy of Idaho. The school now uses Odysseyware as its curriculum provider. With the school change, the staff has remained the same.

Idaho Digital Learning Academy

1303 E. Central Dr.
Suite 200
Meridian, Idaho 83642
United States
Tel: 208.342.0207
Fax: 208.342.1031
Web: idahodigitallearning.org
Email: idla@idla.k12.id.us
Recognition/Accreditation: NWAC
Grade: 1-12
Type: Charter, Free, Public
Diploma: Yes
Cost: Free
If free, where?: Within the state
Teen and/or Adult: Teens

Additional information: Idaho Digital Learning Academy is a well-known online school that has a reputation for offering a quality education. It works in conjunction with the school districts in the state of Idaho and its program is aligned with their state standards.

Idaho Distance Education Academy
PO Box 338
606 South Ave
Deary, Idaho 83823
United States
Tel: 208.457.1019
Fax: 208.877.1713
Web: www.idahoidea.org
Email: deborahpence@idahoidea.org
Recognition/Accreditation: Idaho State Department of Education
Grade: 1-12
Type: Charter, Free, Public
Diploma: Yes
Cost: Free
If free, where?: Within the state
Teen and/or Adult: Teens
Additional information: More than many other online schools, the idea behind Idaho Distance Education Academy is that the parent plays an important role in their child's education. The school offers parents a wide variety of curriculum from which to choose for their students.

Idaho Virtual Academy
1965 S. Eagle Road
Suite 190
Meridian, Idaho 83642
United States
Tel: 866.339.9066

Fax: 208.322.3688
Web: www.K12.com/idva/
Email: info@idahova.org
Recognition/Accreditation: NWAC
Grade: 3-12
Type: Charter, Free, Public
Diploma: Yes
Cost: Free
If free, where?: Within the state
Teen and/or Adult: Teens
Additional information: Idaho Virtual Academy utilizes the curriculum offers from K12, Inc. It offers an Advanced Learner program and has computers available to borrow. Students earn a high school diploma that meets all state requirements.

Inspire: Idaho Connections Academy
600 N. Steelhead Way, Suite 164
Boise, Idaho 83704
United States
Tel: 208.322.4002
Fax: 208.322.4008
Web: www.connectionsacademy.com/idaho-school
Email: info@connectionsacademy.com
Recognition/Accreditation: NWAC, AdvancED
Grade: 1-12
Type: Charter, Free, Public
Diploma: Yes
Cost: Free
If free, where?: Within the state
Teen and/or Adult: Teens
Additional information: Inspire: Idaho Connections Academy is part of the Connections Academy family of schools. It is a free online public

school available to students throughout the state.

iSucceed Virtual High School
6148 N. Discovery Way Suite 120
Boise, Idaho 83713
United States
Tel: 800.211.1687
Fax: 208.375.3117
Web: isucceed.insightschools.net/
Email: info@isucceedvhs.net
Recognition/Accreditation: NWAC
Grade: 9-12
Type: Charter, Free, Public
Diploma: Yes
Cost: Free
If free, where?: Within the state
Teen and/or Adult: To age 21
Additional information: iSucceed Virtual High School was part of the Insight Schools chain that has been purchased by K12 Inc. In additional to core courses, it also offered Advanced Placement as well as vocational and skill-building courses. For qualified students, there is the possibility to earn college credit based on successful completion.

Richard McKenna Charter High School
675 South Haskett Street
Mountain Home, Idaho 83647
United States
Tel: 208.580.2449 / 888.580.2449
Fax: 208.580.2450
Web: www.rmckenna.org
Email: lcrenshaw@idvhs.org
Recognition/Accreditation: NWAC
Grade: 9-12
Type: Charter, Free, Public
Diploma: Yes

Cost: Free
If free, where?: Within the state
Teen and/or Adult: Teens
Additional information: Richard McKenna Charter High School is an Idaho public charter school. In order to attend, students must have completed the eighth grade and pre-algebra.

Chicago Virtual Charter School

c/o Merit School of Music
38 S. Peoria
Chicago, Illinois 60607
United States
Tel: 866.612.1451
Web: www.K12.com/cvcs/
Email: info@chicagovcs.org
Recognition/Accreditation: Chicago Public Schools
Grade: 1-12
Type: Charter, Free, Public
Diploma: Yes
Cost: Free
If free, where?: Illinois
Teen and/or Adult: Teens
Additional information: Chicago Virtual Charter School utilizes curriculum from K^{12}, Inc. It offers an Advanced Learner Program and has computers available to borrow.

Hadley School for the Blind

700 Elm Street
Winnetka, Illinois 60093
United States
Tel: 847.446.8111
Fax: 847.446.0855
Web: hadley.edu/2_c_HS.asp
Email: info@hadley.edu

Recognition/Accreditation: NCA, DETC
Grade: 9-12
Type: Free, Public
Diploma: Yes
Cost: Free
If free, where?:
Teen and/or Adult: Both
Additional information: Hadley's High School Program allows students to take individual courses or to earn an entire high school diploma. In order to enroll, you must be fourteen and blind (or meet certain vision eligibility requirements).

Hoosier Academies
5640 Caito Drive
Indianapolis, Indiana 46226
United States
Tel: 317.547.1400
Fax: 317.547.1500
Web: www.K12.com/ha/
Email: generalinfo@hoosieracademy.org
Recognition/Accreditation: Indiana Department of Education, Ball State University
Grade: 1-12
Type: Charter, Free, Public
Diploma: Yes
Cost: Free
If free, where?: Within the state
Teen and/or Adult: Teens
Additional information: Hoosier Academies offers three schools: hybrid schools in both Indianapolis and Muncie as well as a fully online school. It is a public charter school authorized by Ball State University. It utilizes the K^{12}, Inc. curriculum.

Iowa Learning Online
Iowa Department of Education
Iowa
United States
Tel: 515-419-3275
Web: www.iowalearningonline.org
Email: gwen.nagel@iowa.gov
Recognition/Accreditation: Iowa Department of Education
Grade: 9-12
Type: Free, Public
Diploma: No
Cost: Free
If free, where?: Within the state
Teen and/or Adult: Teens
Additional information: Iowa Learning Online is designed to help local Iowa school districts expand learning opportunities for their high school students using online courses. Students enroll in ILO courses through their local school district. Each student must be supported locally by a coach.

Iowa Online AP Academy
600 Blank Honors Center
The University of Iowa
Iowa City, Iowa 52242-0454
United States
Tel: 800.336.6463
Fax: 319.335.5151
Web: iowaapacademy.org
Email: Clar-Baldus@uiowa.edu
Recognition/Accreditation: Iowa Department of Education
Grade: 9-12
Type: Free, Public
Diploma: No
Cost: Free

If free, where?: Within the district
Teen and/or Adult: Teens
Additional information: Iowa Online AP Academy offers only Advanced Placement courses. It is primarily for rural and small districts in Iowa.

Insight School of Kansas

16740 W. 175th Street
Olathe, Kansas 66062
United States
Tel: 800.260.0438
Fax: 866.664.2796
Web: ks.insightschools.net
Email: info@insightks.net
Recognition/Accreditation: NWAC
Grade: 9-12
Type: Charter, Free, Public
Diploma: Yes
Cost: Free
If free, where?: Within the state
Teen and/or Adult: Teens
Additional information: Insight School of Kansas is part of the K12, Inc. chain of schools. It offers Honors and Advanced Placement courses. The school offers more than 120 courses.

iQ Academy Kansas

901 Poyntz Avenue
Manhattan, Kansas 66502
United States
Tel: 877.345.4757
Fax: 888.472.8010
Web: iqacademyks.com
Email: info@iqacademyks.com
Recognition/Accreditation: Manhattan-Ogden USD 383
Grade: 7-12

Type: Charter, Free, Public
Diploma: Yes
Cost: Free
If free, where?: Within the state
Teen and/or Adult: Both
Additional information: iQ Academy Kansas is part of the K^{12}, Inc. chain of schools. Students are given access to computers. The school offers eighty courses including Advanced Placement and foreign languages.

Lawrence Virtual School

1104 East 1000 Road
Lawrence, Kansas 66047
United States
Tel: 785.832.5620
Fax: 785.832.5621
Web: www.lawrencevs.org
Email: jrego@usd497.org
Recognition/Accreditation: Lawrence USD 497
Grade: 1-12
Type: Free, Public
Diploma: Yes
Cost: Free
If free, where?: Within the state
Teen and/or Adult: Teens
Additional information: Laurence Virtual School utilizes the K^{12}, Inc. curriculum and offers individualized support for its' students.

Smoky Valley Virtual Charter School

121 South Main
Lindsborg, Kansas 67456
United States
Tel: 785.906.0145
Web:

www.smokyvalley.org/charter/SVVCS/Welcome.html

Email: melmquist@smokyvalley.org
Recognition/Accreditation: Kansas Department of Education
Grade: 9-12
Type: Charter, Free, Public
Diploma: Yes
Cost: Free
If free, where?: Within the state
Teen and/or Adult: Both
Additional information: Smoky Valley Virtual Charter School offers a program for students who need to complete and gain credits to graduate from high school. While it does offer traditional courses, it has a strong focus on credit recovery.

Barren Academy of Virtual and Expanded Learning

202 W. Washington Street
Glasgow, Kentucky 42141
United States
Tel: 270.670.3739
Fax: 270.651.8836
Web: local.barren.kyschools.us/bavel/
Email: amanda.wright@barren.kyschools.us
Recognition/Accreditation: Kentucky Department of Education
Grade: 9-12
Type: Free, Public
Diploma: Yes
Cost: Free
If free, where?: Within the state
Teen and/or Adult: Teens
Additional information: The Barren Academy of Virtual and Expanded Learning (BAVEL) utilizes curriculum from a variety of sources including

Pearson Virtual Learning/Florida Virtual School, Kentucky Virtual High School, and others. It also has partnerships with three Kentucky colleges.

Kentucky Virtual High School
500 Mero Street, 19th Floor CPT
Frankfort, Kentucky 40601
United States
Tel: 502.564.4772 or 866.432.0008
Web: www.kyvs.org
Email: kvhsinquiry@education.ky.gov
Recognition/Accreditation: Kentucky Board of Education
Grade: 9-12
Type: Free, Public
Diploma: Yes
Cost: Free
If free, where?: Within the state
Teen and/or Adult: Teens
Additional information: Kentucky Virtual High School offers a variety of courses including access to an expanded curriculum for all Kentucky students. KVHS offers Advanced Placement and foreign languages. In addition, Kentucky Virtual High School offers multiple credit recovery options.

Louisiana Virtual Charter Academy
1477 Louisiana Avenue
New Orleans, Louisiana 70115
United States
Tel: 504.322.7543
Web: www.K12.com/lavca/
Email: On website
Recognition/Accreditation: Community School for Apprenticeship Learning
Grade: 1-12
Type: Charter, Free, Public

Diploma: Yes
Cost: Free
If free, where?: Within the state
Teen and/or Adult: Teens
Additional information: Louisiana Virtual Charter Academy utilizes the curriculum from K12, Inc. Books and materials are provided to the students. The school provides opportunities for students to participate in school outings.

Louisiana Virtual School
Louisiana Department of Education
Louisiana
United States
Tel: 225.219.0436
Web: www.louisianavirtualschool.net
Email: Sandy.Huval@LA.Gov
Recognition/Accreditation: Louisiana Department of Education
Grade: 9-12
Type: Free, Public
Diploma: Yes
Cost: Free
If free, where?: Within the state
Teen and/or Adult: Teens
Additional information: The Louisiana Virtual School is the result of a partnership between The Louisiana Department of Education and The Louisiana School for Math, Science, and the Arts. Louisiana Virtual School provides students with online courses that meet the Louisiana State Standards.

The VHS Collaborative
4 Clock Tower Place, Suite 510
Maynard, Massachusetts 01754
United States

Tel: 978.897.1900
Fax: 978.897.9839
Web: thevhscollaborative.org
Email: On website
Recognition/Accreditation: NWAC, MSA
Grade: 7-12
Type: Free, Private
Diploma: Yes
Cost: $450 per course (or free)
Teen and/or Adult: Teens
Additional information: Students may be able to take advantage of online courses at The VHS Collaborative at their public school, but it also offers individual courses to students. The VHS Collaborative is better described as a group of teachers providing online instruction. You could be taking an online course at your public high school, but the teacher actually works at a different school. Courses might be free if paid for by public school.

Fusion Academy of Michigan
15250 Grand River Avenue
Detroit, Michigan 48227
United States
Tel: 313.452.3901
Web: www.ombudsman.com/FusionHome.aspx
Email:
Recognition/Accreditation: AdvancED, MSA
Grade: 9-12
Type: Charter, Free, Public
Diploma: Yes
Cost: Free
If free, where?:
Teen and/or Adult: To age 21
Additional information: Fusion Academy of Michigan is jointly operated by Connections Education and Ombudsman. In the beginning,

students work with the digital content at one of its campuses, but good academic performance earns the student the right to check out a laptop and do some of the online work from home.

Michigan Connections Academy
2140 University Park Drive, Suite 270
Okemos, Michigan 48864
United States
Tel: 517.507.5390
Fax: 517.507.5389
Web: www.connectionsacademy.com/michigan-school/home.aspx
Email: info@connectionsacademy.com
Recognition/Accreditation: AdvancED
Grade: 1-12
Type: Charter, Free, Public
Diploma: Yes
Cost: Free
If free, where?: Within the state
Teen and/or Adult: Teens
Additional information: Michigan Connections Academy is part of the Connections Academy family of schools. In addition to a solid academic grounding, the school offers a wide array of clubs and activities that are available to all students.

Michigan Virtual Charter Academy
678 Front Avenue, NW
Grand Rapids, Michigan 49504
United States
Tel: 877.794.9422
Web: www.K12.com/mvca/
Email: On website
Recognition/Accreditation: Grand Valley State University
Grade: 1-12

Type: Charter, Free, Public
Diploma: Yes
Cost: Free
If free, where?: Within the state
Teen and/or Adult: Teens
Additional information: Michigan Virtual Charter Academy utilizes digital curriculum from K^{12}, Inc. It is an online charter school authorized by the Grand Valley State University.

Michigan Virtual High School
3101 Technology Blvd., Suite G
Lansing, Michigan 48910
United States
Tel: 888.532.5806
Fax: 517.336.7787
Web: www.mivhs.org
Email: mivuhelp@mivu.org
Recognition/Accreditation: NCA
Grade: 6-12
Type: Free, Public
Diploma: Yes
Cost: Free if your home school will pay.
Teen and/or Adult: Teens
Additional information: Michigan Virtual High School has been offering online courses for over a dozen years to a variety of students including those with Advanced Placement, credit recovery, homeschoolers, and others. Michigan Virtual High School is operated by the Michigan Virtual University.

Virtual Learning Academy of St. Clair County
PO Box 1500
Marysville, Michigan 48040
United States

Tel: 810.455.4025 / 810.364.8990
Fax: 810.364.5315
Web:
www.sccresa.org/countyeducation/academies/virt
uallearningacademy/
Email: lapish.denice@sccresa.org
Recognition/Accreditation: St. Clair County
RESA
Grade: 9-12
Type: Charter, Free, Public
Diploma: Yes
Cost: Free
If free, where?: Within the county
Teen and/or Adult: To age 21
Additional information: Virtual Learning
Academy of St. Clair County accepts two types of
students. First, it accepts students who are ages 16
-19 who have stopped attending school for more
than thirty days. The second group are expelled
public school students in grades 9 - 12.

Westwood Cyber High School
25824 Michigan
Inkster, Michigan 48141
United States
Tel: 313.565.0288 / 313.565.0288
Web: westwood.chs.schooldesk.net
Recognition/Accreditation: NCA
Grade: 9-12
Type: Public
Diploma: Yes
Cost: Free
If free, where?: Within the state
Teen and/or Adult: Teens
Additional information: Westwood Cyber High
School has a seat-time waiver. It is funded by the
Michigan Department of Education to work with at-

risk youth. Students must have completed at least eighth grade in order to be admitted and the school is only for students who are ages 14 - 19.

BlueSky Online School
33 Wentworth Avenue E
Suite 300
West Saint Paul, Minnesota 55118
United States
Tel: 651.642.0888
Fax: 651.642.0435
Web: www.blueskyschool.org
Email: info@blueskyschool.org
Recognition/Accreditation: Minnesota Department of Education
Grade: 7-12
Type: Charter, Free, Public
Diploma: Yes
Cost: Free
If free, where?: Within the state
Teen and/or Adult: Teens
Additional information: BlueSky Online School is an online public charter school for students in Minnesota. BlueSky has a variety of students including high-achievers, teen parents, students who need to work, and others.

Insight School of Minnesota
6870 Shingle Creek Pkwy., B112
Brooklyn Center, Minnesota 55430
United States
Tel: 800.711.5944
Fax: 866.366.0177
Web: mn.insightschools.net
Email: info@insightmn.net
Recognition/Accreditation: NWAC
Grade: 9-12

Type: Charter, Free, Public
Diploma: Yes
Cost: Free
If free, where?: Within the state
Teen and/or Adult: Teens
Additional information: Insight School of Minnesota is part of the K12, Inc. chain of online schools. In addition to its core courses, it also offers Advanced Placement and vocational courses.

iQ Academy Minnesota
1519 Pebble Lake Road
Fergus Falls, Minnesota 56537
United States
Tel: 877.994.4766
Fax: 218.998.3952
Web: iqacademymn.org
Email: info@iqacademymn.org
Recognition/Accreditation: Independent School District 544
Grade: 6-12
Type: Charter, Free, Public
Diploma: Yes
Cost: Free
If free, where?: Within the state
Teen and/or Adult: To age 21
Additional information: iQ Academy is part of the iQ Academy chain of schools. It offers instruction for grades 6-12. It utilizes teachers licensed by the state of Minnesota. iQ Academy also offers clubs and local events. It was Minnesota's first accredited 6-12 online school.

Minnesota Online High School
1313 Fifth Street, SE, Suite 300
Minneapolis, Minnesota 55414
United States

Tel: 800.764.8166
Fax: 866.586.2870
Web: www.mnohs.org
Email: info@mnohs.org
Recognition/Accreditation: Minnesota Department of Education
Grade: 9-12
Type: Charter, Free, Public
Diploma: Yes
Cost: Free
If free, where?: Minnesota students only
Teen and/or Adult: Teens
Additional information: Minnesota Online High School (MNOHS) uses curriculum developed byt the teachers at the school. The school prides itself on its small class sizes and its advisory curriculum that guides students in their move toward being successful with online courses.

Minnesota Virtual Academy
306 West Elm Street
Houston, Minnesota 55943
United States
Tel: 866.215.2292
Fax: 800.451.6036
Web: mnva.k12.mn.us/se3bin/clientschool.cgi?schoolname=school189
Email: info@mnva.k12.mn.us
Recognition/Accreditation: Houston Public Schools
Grade: 1-12
Type: Charter, Free, Public
Diploma: Yes
Cost: Free
If free, where?: Within the state
Teen and/or Adult: Teens

Additional information: Minnesota Virtual Academy is expanding to include a high school option. The curriculum is provided by K[12], Inc.. It is part of the Houston Public Schools system and is the largest K-12 online school in the state of Minnesota.

Minnesota Virtual High School
Minnesota
United States
Tel: 866.356.5873
Web:
minnesotavirtualhighschool.com/index.html
Recognition/Accreditation: NCA
Grade: 6-12
Type: Charter, Free, Public
Diploma: Yes
Cost: Free
If free, where?: Within the state
Teen and/or Adult: To age 21
Additional information: Minnesota Virtual High School is a program of Minnesota Transitions Charter School. It utilizes teachers certified by the state of Minnesota. Minnesota Virtual High School utilizes the well-known Advanced Academics curriculum.

MTS Minnesota Connections Academy
1336 Energy Park Drive Suite 100
St. Paul, Minnesota 55108
United States
Tel: 651.523.0888
Fax: 651.726.2917
Web:
www.connectionsacademy.com/minnesota-school/home.aspx
Email: mnelson@connectionsacademy.com

Recognition/Accreditation: NCA
Grade: 1-12
Type: Charter, Free, Public
Diploma: Yes
Cost: Free
If free, where?: Within the state
Teen and/or Adult: Teens
Additional information: MTS Minnesota Connections Academy (MTSMCA), a tuition-free online public school, is part of the Connections Education chain of schools. For grades 6-12, computers are available for loan to students and subsidies are given for Internet connections.

Wolf Creek Online High School

13750 Lake Blvd
Lindstrom, Minnesota 55045
United States
Tel: 651.213.2095
Fax: 651.257.0576
Web: wolfcreek.chisagolakes.k12.mn.us
Email: tquarnstrom@chisagolakes.k12.mn.us
Recognition/Accreditation: NCA
Grade: 9-12
Type: Charter, Free, Public
Diploma: Yes
Cost: Free
If free, where?: Within the state
Teen and/or Adult: To age 21
Additional information: Wolf Creek Online High School is a hybrid program. The school recommends that students attend a minimum of five hours per week (in addition to the time spent on courses at home). The school's philosophy is what they call "small community." Students are assisted by a learning manager for both the

academic and non-academic components.

Missouri Virtual Instruction Program
205 Jefferson St., 7th Floor P.O. Box 480
Jefferson, Missouri 65102
United States
Tel: 573.751.2453
Fax: 573.522.1134
Web: www.movip.org/
Email: MoVIP@nwmissouri.edu
Recognition/Accreditation: Missouri
Department of Elementary and Secondary
Education
Grade: 1-12
Type: Free, Public
Diploma: No
Cost: Free
If free, where?: Within the state
Teen and/or Adult: Teens
Additional information: MoVIP is the state
virtual school for Missouri and offers courses to
students in grades K-12. One group of students for
this school are Missouri students who need
advanced courses or foreign language courses not
offered at their traditional high schools. MoVIP
offers 172 different online courses.

SLPS Virtual School
801 N. 11th Street
St. Louis, Missouri 63101
United States
Tel: 314-231-3720
Web: www.slps.org/slps/site/default.asp
Email: Kesha.Chatman@slps.org
Recognition/Accreditation: Saint Louis
Public Schools
Grade: 1-12

Type: Charter, Free, Public
Diploma: Yes
Cost: Free
If free, where?: Within the district
Teen and/or Adult: Teens
Additional information: In partnership with Kaplan Virtual Education, this school is part of St. Louis Public Schools. There are some face-to-face weekly meetings that are a requirement. A student must be a resident of the area served by the Saint Louis Public Schools in order to be eligible.

Montana Digital Academy
The University of Montana
32 Campus Drive
Missoula, Montana 59812
United States
Tel: 406.243.4619
Fax: 406.243.5494
Web: montanadigitalacademy.org
Email:
robert.currie@montanadigitalacademy.org
Recognition/Accreditation: University of Montana
Grade: 9-12
Type: Public
Diploma: No
Teen and/or Adult: Teens
Additional information: Montana Digital Academy offers dual credit via the Montana University System. It offers Advanced Placement courses as well as elective courses that may not be available at a student's traditional high school. Homeschoolers will need to register for MTDA courses at their local public school.

Beacon Academy of Nevada
8970 W. Tropicana Avenue
Suite 6
Las Vegas, Nevada 89147
United States
Tel: 877.994.8910
Fax: 866.396.8910
Web: beaconacademynv.org
Email: info@beaconacademynv.org
Recognition/Accreditation: Nevada Board of Education
Grade: 9-12
Type: Charter, Free, Public
Diploma: Yes
Cost: Free
If free, where?: Nevada
Teen and/or Adult: To age 21
Additional information: Beacon Academy of Nevada offers over 130 online courses including Advanced Placement and honors courses. Students work with the counseling staff to choose the right courses. Full-time students may borrow laptop computer. It also has credit recovery options available.

Carson Online
Nevada
United States
Tel: 877.380.4813
Web: www.carsononlineschool.com
Recognition/Accreditation: Carson City School District
Grade: 6-12
Type: Charter, Free, Public
Diploma: Yes
Cost: Free

If free, where?: Surrounding counties
Teen and/or Adult: Teens
Additional information: Carson Online utilizes the Advanced Academics curriculum. It serves students in the counties of Carson City, Churchill, Douglas, Lyon, Mineral, Storey, and Washoe.

Nevada Connections Academy
175 Salomon Circle, Suite 201
Sparks, Nevada 89434
United States
Tel: 775.826.4200
Fax: 775.826.4288
Web: www.connectionsacademy.com/nevada-school/home.aspx
Email: cwhite@connectionsacademy.com
Recognition/Accreditation: NWAC, AdvancED
Grade: 1-12
Type: Charter, Free, Public
Diploma: Yes
Cost: Free
If free, where?: Within the state
Teen and/or Adult: Teens
Additional information: Nevada Connections Academy (NCA) is part of the Connections Education family of schools. It serves students in grades K-12. Nevada Connections Academy accepts students throughout the state of Nevada.

Nevada Virtual Academy
8965 South Eastern Avenue
Suite 330
Las Vegas, Nevada 89123
United States
Tel: 866.912.3350
Fax: 702.407.5055

Web: www.K12.com/nvva
Email: administration@nvva.org
Recognition/Accreditation: Nevada Department of Education
Grade: 1-12
Type: Charter, Free, Public
Diploma: Yes
Cost: Free
If free, where?: Within the state
Teen and/or Adult: Teens
Additional information: Nevada Virtual Academy utilizes the K^{12}, Inc. curriculum. It offers a rigorous advanced learners program as well as a wide variety of extracurricular activities.

Odyssey Charter High School
2251 S. Jones Blvd
Las Vegas, Nevada 89146
United States
Tel: 702.257.0578
Fax: 702.312.3260
Web: www.odysseyk12.org
Email: info@odysseyk12.org
Recognition/Accreditation: NWAC
Grade: 1-12
Type: Charter, Free, Public
Diploma: Yes
Cost: Free
If free, where?: Within the county
Teen and/or Adult: Teens
Additional information: Odyssey Charter Schools is the largest online charter school in Nevada. It uses a blended learning model that requires both in-person instruction and online learning. It is chartered by the Clark County School District.

Washoe Online Learning for the Future
785 W. Sixth Street
Reno, Nevada 89503
United States
Tel: 774.333.6100
Fax: 775.333.5189
Web: www.wolflearning.com/washoe/home.aspx
Email: On Website
Recognition/Accreditation: NCA
Grade: 1-12
Type: Free, Public
Diploma: Yes
Cost: Free
If free, where?: Within the county
Teen and/or Adult: Teens
Additional information: Washoe Online Learning for the Future is a program of the Washoe County School District. This online school utilizes the Connections Education curriculum.

Virtual Learning Academy Charter School
30 Linden Street
Exeter, New Hampshire 03833
United States
Tel: 603.778.2500
Fax: 866.651.5038
Web: www.vlacs.org
Email: info@vlacs.org
Recognition/Accreditation: New Hampshire Board of Education
Grade: 9-12
Type: Charter, Free, Public
Diploma: Yes
Cost: Free
If free, where?: Within the state
Teen and/or Adult: Teens

Additional information: Virtual Learning Academy Charter School is an approved New Hampshire public school. It offers free online courses throughout the state. The school accepts both full-time and part-time students.

New Jersey Virtual Academy Charter School
180 William Street
Newark, New Jersey 07103
United States
Tel: 855.652.3926
Web: www.K12.com/njvacs
Email: info@njvacs.org
Recognition/Accreditation:
Grade: 1-12
Type: Charter, Free, Public
Diploma: Yes
Cost: Free
Teen and/or Adult: Teens
Additional information: The New Jersey Department of Education (DOE) announced on Monday, July 16, 2012 that it would not grant a charter to New Jersey Virtual Academy Charter School (NJVACS) for the 2012–2013 school year. Instead, New Jersey Virtual Academy Charter School asked for another planning year for the school.

New Mexico Virtual Academy
845 North Sullivan
Farmington, New Mexico 87401
United States
Tel: 855.718.7724
Web: www.K12.com/nmva
Email: ltodd@K12.com
Recognition/Accreditation: On website

Grade: 6-12, 7-12, 7-8, 9-12
Type: Charter, Free, Public
Diploma: Yes
Cost: Free
Teen and/or Adult: Teens
Additional information: New Mexico Virtual Academy includes a blended learning component at its Farmington Learning Center. It utilizes the digital curriculum from K^{12}, Inc. The school loans computers to students who need them.

Centre for Distance Learning and Innovation

Department of Education
PO Box 8700
St. John's, Newfoundland A1B 4J6
United States
Tel: 709.729.7614
Fax: 709.729.7614
Web: www.cdli.ca
Email: jpaul@cdli.ca
Recognition/Accreditation: Provincial Authority
Grade: 1-12
Type: Public
Diploma: Yes
Cost: Free
If free, where?: Newfoundland
Teen and/or Adult: Teens
Additional information: In previous years, in this Canadian province, distance learning programs were entirely print. They have moved to online versions to allow for ease in making changes to the curriculum.

North Carolina Virtual Public School

1017 Main Campus Drive Partners I Bldg, Room

1610
Raleigh, North Carolina 27606
United States
Tel: 919.513.8550
Fax: 919.513.2557
Web: www.ncvps.org
Email: ncvps@dpi.state.nc.us
Recognition/Accreditation: North Carolina
Department of Public Instruction
Grade: 1-12
Type: Free, Public
Diploma: No
Cost: Free
If free, where?: Within the state
Teen and/or Adult: Teens
Additional information: North Carolina Virtual
Public School is a service of the state of North
Carolina. In addition to credit recovery
opportunities, the school offers expanded options
for North Carolina students including Advanced
Placement, honors, and world languages.

Electronic Classroom of Tomorrow
3700 S. High Street
Suite 95
Columbus, Ohio 43207
United States
Tel: 888.326.8395
Web: www.ecotohio.org
Email: info@ecotoh.org
Recognition/Accreditation: NCA
Grade: 1-12
Type: Charter, Free, Public
Diploma: Yes
Cost: Free
If free, where?: Ohio
Teen and/or Adult: Teens

Additional information: Electronic Classroom of Tomorrow (ECOT) was the first online school to begin operating in Ohio. It remains quite popular with over 10,000 currently enrolled students and over 5,000 graduates. ECOT also provides students with computers on an as-needed basis.

iLearnOhio
Ohio
United States
Web: www.ilearnohio.org
Email: On website
Recognition/Accreditation:
Grade: 1-12
Type: Free, Public
Diploma: Yes
Cost: Fee waivers are available
Teen and/or Adult: Teens
Additional information: Unlike other programs, iLearnOhio is actually a virtual clearinghouse of online courses provided by various providers. It is administered by The Ohio State University's Ohio Resource Center. Most of the courses currently available from iLearnOhio are online Advanced Placement courses.

Ohio Connections Academy
2727 Madison Rd, Suite 302
Cincinnati, Ohio 45209
United States
Tel: 614.840.9401 ext. 312
Fax: 513.533.3260
Web: www.connectionsacademy.com/ohio-school/home.aspx
Email: rlambert@connectionsacademy.com
Recognition/Accreditation: NCA
Grade: 1-12

Type: Charter, Free, Public
Diploma: Yes
Cost: Free
If free, where?: Within the state
Teen and/or Adult: Teens
Additional information: The Ohio Department of Education rated Ohio Connections Academy as "Excellent" in 2010. It was the only eSchool so rated. Ohio Connections Academy is part of the Connections Education family of schools.

Ohio Distance & Electronic Learning Academy
121 South Main Street, Suite 102
Akron, Ohio 44308
United States
Tel: 330.253.8680
Fax: 800.514.8227
Web: www.ohdela.com
Email: ohdela.info@ohdela.com
Recognition/Accreditation: Ohio Charter School Council
Grade: 1-12
Type: Charter, Free, Public
Diploma: Yes
Cost: Free
If free, where?: Within the state
Teen and/or Adult: Teens
Additional information: In addition to online courses, OHDELA students go on field trips, have a student council and have a chapter of the National Honor Society. The school's students score higher on achievement tests than traditional schools.

Ohio Virtual Academy
1655 Holland Road, Suite F
Maumee, Ohio 43537

United States
Tel: 877.648.2512
Fax: 419.482.0954
Web: www.K12.com/ohva/
Email: info@ohva.org
Recognition/Accreditation: NCA, AdvancED
Grade: 1-12
Type: Charter, Free, Public
Diploma: Yes
Cost: Free
If free, where?: Within the state
Teen and/or Adult: Teens
Additional information: Ohio Virtual Academy utilizes digital curriculum from K12. In addition to an advanced learner program, it also offers a number of academic enrichment activities.

QDA
400 Mill Avenue SE
Suite 901
New Philadelphia, Ohio 44663
United States
Tel: 866.968.7032
Web: www.go2qda.org/qda/site/default.asp
Email: applications@go2qda.org
Recognition/Accreditation: Ohio Department of Education
Grade: 1-12
Type: Free, Public
Diploma: Yes
Cost: Free
If free, where?: Within the state
Teen and/or Adult: Teens
Additional information: QDA offers both Internet-based and textbook-based instruction based on the needs of the student. It is a state-wide effort where all students are provided with a

computer, Internet connection, and textbooks.

TRECA Digital Academy
100 Executive Drive
Marion, Ohio 43302
United States
Tel: 800.567.1686
Fax: 740.389.6695
Web: www.tda.treca.org
Email: admissions@treca.org
Recognition/Accreditation: Ohio Department of Education
Grade: 1-12
Type: Charter, Free, Public
Diploma: Yes
Cost: Free
If free, where?: Within the state
Teen and/or Adult: Teens
Additional information: TRECA Digital Academy (TDA) is an online K-12 school that is open to all Ohio public school districts. Students have the opportunity to progress at their own pace. Utilizes today's technology in ways that allow students to progress at their own pace. Courses meet all of the Ohio achievement standards.

Virtual Community School of Ohio
4480 Refugee Road
Suite 304
Columbus, Ohio 43232
United States
Tel: 614.501.9473 / 866-501-9473
Fax: 614.501.9470
Web: www.vcslearn.org
Email: info@vcslearn.org
Recognition/Accreditation: Ohio Department

of Education
Grade: 1-12
Type: Charter, Free, Public
Diploma: Yes
Cost: Free
If free, where?: Within the state
Teen and/or Adult: Teens
Additional information: Students at Virtual Community School of Ohio are provided with a free computer, printer, scanner, and Internet access as long as they are enrolled in the program. The virtual school is open to any students who meet certain age, grade, and geographic enrollment criteria.

Oklahoma Virtual Charter Academy
PO Box 4490
Nicoma Park, Oklahoma 73066
United States
Tel: 866.467.0848
Fax: 405.259.8332
Web: www.K12.com/ovca
Email: ovca.media@K12.com
Recognition/Accreditation: Choctaw-Nicoma Park School District
Grade: 1-12
Type: Charter, Free, Public
Diploma: Yes
Cost: Free
If free, where?: Within the state
Teen and/or Adult: Teens
Additional information: Oklahoma Virtual Charter Academy utilizes curriculum from K12, Inc. Teachers all possess Oklahoma teacher certification.

Oklahoma Virtual High School
Oklahoma

United States
Tel: 888.425.7178
Web: www.oklahomavirtualhighschool.com
Email: On website
Recognition/Accreditation: NCA
Grade: 6-12
Type: Charter, Free, Public
Diploma: Yes
Cost: Free
If free, where?: Within the state
Teen and/or Adult: To age 21
Additional information: Oklahoma Virtual High School uses the Advanced Academics curriculum. In addition to the free option, OVHS also offers fee-based courses for students who are over age 21 or who are not interested in a full-time option.

OSU K-12 Distance Learning Academy
Oklahoma State University
K-12 Distance Learning Academy LSE 213
Stillwater, Oklahoma
United States
Tel: 888.824.5147
Web: k12.okstate.edu
Email: k12-osu@okstate.edu
Recognition/Accreditation: Oklahoma State University
Grade: 1-12
Type: Public
Diploma: No
Teen and/or Adult: Teens
Additional information: OSU K-12 Distance Learning Academy utilizes interactive technology in its online courses for grades K-12. Tutors and instructors are available via a toll-free phone number.

Clackamas Web Academy
8740 SE Sunnybrook Blvd., Suite #350
Clackamas, Oregon 97015
United States
Tel: 503.659.4664
Fax: 503.659.4994
Web: clackamaswebacademy.org
Email: linnb@clackweb.org
Recognition/Accreditation: NWAC
Grade: 1-12
Type: Charter, Free, Public
Diploma: Yes
Cost: Free
If free, where?: Oregon
Teen and/or Adult: Teens
Additional information: Clackamas Web Academy is a combination of online curriculum and one-to-one teaching in the home. In addition to online courses, Clackamas Web Academy provides opportunities to volunteer in the community, complete internships, and earn college credits.

Insight School of Oregon
309 SW 6th Ave, Suite 820
Portland, Oregon 97204
United States
Tel: (800) 711-0763
Fax: (866) 529-1480
Web: or.insightschools.net
Email: info@insightor.net
Recognition/Accreditation: NWAC
Grade: 9-12
Type: Charter, Free, Public
Diploma: Yes
Cost: Free
If free, where?: Within the state
Teen and/or Adult: Teens

Additional information: Insight Schools is now part of the K¹², Inc. family of schools. It offers more than 120 courses including foundation, core, and advanced online courses for its' students.

Oregon Connections Academy
38761 North Main St.
Scio, Oregon 97374
United States
Tel: 503.394.4315
Fax: 503.394.4320
Web: www.connectionsacademy.com/oregon-school/home.aspx
Email: jwilks@connectionsacademy.com
Recognition/Accreditation: NWAC, AdvancED
Grade: 1-12
Type: Charter, Free, Public
Diploma: Yes
Cost: Free
If free, where?: Within the state
Teen and/or Adult: Teens
Additional information: Oregon Connections Academy (ORCA) is part of the Connections Education family of schools. Students who are in grades K-8 can borrow computers.

Oregon State University K-12 Online
4943 The Valley Library
Corvallis, Oregon 97331
United States
Tel: 800.667.1465
Web: k12online.oregonstate.edu
Email: tryna.luton@oregonstate.edu
Recognition/Accreditation: NWAC
Grade: 1-12
Type: Public

Diploma: No
Teen and/or Adult: Teens
Additional information: Not currently offering courses.

Oregon Virtual Academy
400 Virginia Avenue
Suite 210
North Bend, Oregon 97459
United States
Tel: 866.529.0160
Fax: 866.991.3018
Web: www.K12.com/orva/home
Email: On website
Recognition/Accreditation: North Bend School District
Grade: 1-12
Type: Charter, Free, Public
Diploma: Yes
Cost: Free
If free, where?: Within the state
Teen and/or Adult: Teens
Additional information: Oregon Virtual Academy utilizes curriculum from K12, Inc. The school offers a significant number of extracurricular activities for its students.

21st Century Cyber Charter School
805 Springdale Drive
Exton, Pennsylvania 19341
United States
Tel: 484.875.5400
Fax: 484.875.5404
Web: www.21cccs.org
Email: info@21cccs.org
Recognition/Accreditation: Pennsylvania Department of Education

Grade: 6-12
Type: Charter, Free, Public
Diploma: Yes
Cost: Free
If free, where?: Within the state
Teen and/or Adult: Teens
Additional information: 21st Century Cyber Charter School has met Adequate Yearly Progress (AYP) for the last five years. This is the standard used by the federal government in evaluating schools. It is the only online charter school in Pennsylvania which has done so. In addition to the courses, 21st Century Cyber Charter School offers many extracurricular activities including yearbook, clubs, National Honor Society, and more.

Achievement House Charter School
222 Valley Creek Boulevard
Suite 301
Exton, Pennsylvania 19341
United States
Tel: 484.615.6200
Fax: 610.644.7019
Web: achievementcharter.com
Email: drgrande@achievementcharter.com
Recognition/Accreditation: Pennsylvania Department of Education
Grade: 7-12
Type: Charter, Free, Public
Diploma: Yes
Cost: Free
If free, where?: Pennsylvania
Teen and/or Adult: Teens
Additional information: By the 2012-2013 school year, Achievement House Charter School will have expanded to offer programs for students in grades K-12. Students at this school receive real-

time and self-scheduled instruction. Students are provided with laptops and other technology to support their educational efforts.

Agora Cyber Charter School

995 Old Eagle School Road
Suite 315
Wayne, Pennsylvania 19087
United States
Tel: 866.548.9452
Fax: 866.529.0166
Web: www.K12.com/agora
Email: info@agora.org
Recognition/Accreditation: Pennsylvania Department of Education
Grade: 1-12
Type: Charter, Free, Public
Diploma: Yes
Cost: Free
If free, where?: Pennsylvania
Teen and/or Adult: Teens
Additional information: Agora Cyber Charter School is available to K-12 students. The curriculum used is from K12, Inc. The school provides all necessary books, materials, and a computer. The computer is on loan and only for middle and high school students. Students are allowed to participate in their school district's athletics and extracurricular activities programs. Agora has a program for advanced learners.

Commonwealth Connections Academy

4050 Crums Mill Road
Suite 303
Harrisburg, Pennsylvania 17112
United States
Tel: 717.651.7200

Fax: 717.651.0670
Web:
www.connectionsacademy.com/pennsylvania-
school/free-online-public-school.aspx
Email: info@connectionsacademy.com
Recognition/Accreditation: AdvancED, MSA
Grade: 1-12
Type: Charter, Free, Public
Diploma: Yes
Cost: Free
If free, where?: Pennsylvania
Teen and/or Adult: Teens
Additional information: The Commonwealth
Connections Academy (CCA) has an independent
Board of Directors; meetings are open to the public.
Commonwealth Connections Academy is part of the
Connections Education family of schools.

PA Distance Learning Charter School
2200 Georgetowne Drive Suite 300
Sewickley, Pennsylvania 15143
United States
Tel: 724.933.7300
Fax: 866.977.3527
Web: www.padistance.org
Email: On website
Recognition/Accreditation: Pennsylvania
Department of Education
Grade: 1-12
Type: Charter, Free, Public
Diploma: Yes
Cost: Free
If free, where?: Within the state
Teen and/or Adult: Teens
Additional information: The readers of Central
Penn Parent magazine voted PA Distance Learning
one of the best public schools, whether online or

off-line, to send your child. Pennsylvania has very specific time requirements; students log a minimum of 990 total hours. In order to complete the curriculum from PA Distance, a student would need to work for 27.5 hours per week.

PA Learners Online
475 East Waterfront Drive
Homestead, Pennsylvania 15120
United States
Tel: 412.394.5733
Fax: 412.394.4604
Web: www.palearnersonline.com
Email: paloadmissions@aiu3.net
Recognition/Accreditation: Pennsylvania Department of Education
Grade: 1-12
Type: Charter, Free, Public
Diploma: Yes
Cost: Free
If free, where?: Within the state
Teen and/or Adult: Teens
Additional information: PA Learners Online (PALO) is a tuition-free cyber charter school managed by the Allegheny Intermediate Unit 3, a consortium of ten founding school districts.

Pennsylvania Cyber Charter School
1200 Midland Avenue
Midland, Pennsylvania 15059
United States
Tel: 724.643.1180 / 724.643.1180
Fax: 724.643.2845
Web: www.pacyber.org
Email: EnrollmentInfo@pacyber.org
Recognition/Accreditation: Pennsylvania Department of Education

Grade: 1-12
Type: Charter, Free, Public
Diploma: Yes
Cost: Free
If free, where?: Within the state
Teen and/or Adult: Teens
Additional information: Pennsylvania Cyber Charter School prides itself on the customization of the curriculum to match the needs of students. It is a large online school providing education to thousands of students across the state.

Pennsylvania Virtual Charter School
One West Main Street Suite 400
Norristown, Pennsylvania 19401
United States
Tel: 610.275.8500
Fax: 610.275.1719
Web: www.pavcsk12.org
Email: info@pavcsk12.org
Recognition/Accreditation: Pennsylvania Department of Education
Grade: 1-12
Type: Charter, Free, Public
Diploma: Yes
Cost: Free
If free, where?: Within the state
Teen and/or Adult: Teens
Additional information: The Pennsylvania Virtual Charter School (PAVCS) has more than 4,000 students. It utilizes curriculum from K12, Inc. Pennsylvania Virtual Charter School's charter was renewed in 2011 for an additional five years.

SusQ-Cyber Charter School
240 Market Street, Box 1a, Suite 15
Bloomsburg, Pennsylvania 17815

United States
Tel: 570.245.0252 / 866.370.1226
Fax: 570.245.0246
Web: www.susqcyber.org
Email: On website
Recognition/Accreditation: Pennsylvania Department of Education
Grade: 9-12
Type: Charter, Free, Public
Diploma: Yes
Cost: Free
If free, where?: Within the state
Teen and/or Adult: Teens
Additional information: The SusQ-Cyber Charter School was Pennsylvania's first online charter school. While older, it has maintained a smaller student body. Students are provided with a computer and a printer with which to do school work.

Puerto Rico Virtual School
P.O. Box 190759
Hato Rey, Puerto Rico 00919-0759
United States
Tel: 787.773-3586
Web: utc.dde.pr/cursosenlinea/
Email: cel@de.govierno.pr
Recognition/Accreditation: Puerto Rico Department of Education
Grade: 9-12
Type: Public
Diploma: No
Teen and/or Adult: Teens
Additional information: Website is in both English and Spanish. It is unclear where instruction currently stands. Please contact the school for

further information about its academic offerings.

Credenda Virtual High School
PO Box 2950
Prince Albert, Saskatchewan S6V 7M3
Canada
Tel: 306.764.2847
Fax: 306.764.2857
Web: www.credenda.net
Email: registrar@credenda.net
Recognition/Accreditation: Province of Saskatchewan & Prairie Spirit School District
Grade: 9-12
Type: Public
Diploma: Yes
Teen and/or Adult: Teens
Additional information: Credenda Virtual High School serves primarily, but not exclusively, First Nations students in Canada. Unlike a number of other programs, it offers real-time interaction with teachers at specifically scheduled times.

Palmetto State e-Cademy
115 Atrium Way
Suite 200
Columbia, South Carolina 29223
United States
Tel: 888.994.4772
Fax: 803.935.0071
Web: www.psecademy.org
Email: info@PSEcademy.org
Recognition/Accreditation: NWAC
Grade: 9-12
Type: Charter, Free, Public
Diploma: Yes
Cost: Free

If free, where?: Within the state
Teen and/or Adult: To age 21
Additional information: Palmetto State E-cademy is available to the entire state of South Carolina. Each of its core courses has been vetted by the state's Department of Education to ensure that it prepares students for state exams.

Provost Academy South Carolina
400 Arbor Lake Drive, Suite B800
Columbia, South Carolina 29223
United States
Tel: 877.265.3195
Web: sc.provostacademy.com
Email: info@provostacademy.com
Recognition/Accreditation: South Carolina Department of Education
Grade: 9-12
Type: Charter, Free, Public
Diploma: Yes
Cost: Free
If free, where?: South Carolina
Teen and/or Adult: To age 21
Additional information: Provost Academy South Carolina is part of the Provost Academy chain of schools, part of the well-known EdisonLearning. It offers custom learning plans that are tailored to the individual needs of each student.

South Carolina Connections Academy
220 Stoneridge Drive Suite 403
Columbia, South Carolina 29210
United States
Tel: 803.212.4712
Fax: 803.212.4946
Web: www.connectionsacademy.com/south-

carolina-school/FAQs/home.aspx
Email: info@connectionsacademy.com
Recognition/Accreditation: SACS, AdvancED
Grade: 1-12
Type: Charter, Free, Public
Diploma: Yes
Cost: Free
If free, where?: Within the state
Teen and/or Adult: Teens
Additional information: South Carolina Connections Academy (SCCA), a tuition-free online public school, is part of the Connections Education family of schools. South Carolina Connections Academy was South Carolina's first online charter school.

South Carolina Virtual Charter School

140 Stoneridge Drive, Suite 420
Columbia, South Carolina 29210
United States
Tel: 866.467.5186 / 877.253.6279
Fax: 803.253.6279
Web: www.K12.com/scvcs/
Email: smuse@K12.com
Recognition/Accreditation: South Carolina Public Charter School District
Grade: 1-12
Type: Charter, Free, Public
Diploma: Yes
Cost: Free
If free, where?: Within the state
Teen and/or Adult: Teens
Additional information: South Carolina Virtual Charter School utilizes curriculum from K^{12}, Inc. In addition to its core courses, it offers an advanced learner program as well as a wealth of

extracurricular activities including clubs and more.

NSU Center for Statewide E-learning
1200 South Jay Street
Aberdeen, South Dakota 57401
United States
Tel: 605.626.3011
Web:
www.northern.edu/Academics/Departments/E-
Learning/Pages/default.aspx
Email: info@northern.edu
Recognition/Accreditation: Northern State
University
Grade: 1-12
Type: Public
Diploma: No
Cost: Free to students / Some cost to districts
Teen and/or Adult: Teens
Additional information: Part of Northern State
University in South Dakota. Master teachers are
required to hold six office hours per week.

South Dakota Virtual School
South Dakota
United States
Tel: 605.773.3134
Web: sdvs.k12.sd.us
Email: DOESDVirtualSchool@state.sd.us
Recognition/Accreditation: South Dakota
Department of Education
Grade: 9-12
Type: Free, Public
Diploma: No
Cost: Free
If free, where?: South Dakota (but only if your
home school pays)
Teen and/or Adult: Teens

Additional information: South Dakota students who wish to attend South Dakota Virtual School must first register for the program with their home school district. The school is an online program of the South Dakota Department of Education.

Hamilton County Virtual School
3074 Hickory Valley Road
Chattanooga, Tennessee 37421
United States
Tel: 423.209.8804
Fax: 423.209.8801
Web: www.hcde.org/hamilton-county-schools/alternative-programs/hamilton-county-virtual-school
Email: hcvs@hcde.org
Recognition/Accreditation: Hamilton County Department of Education
Grade: 1-12
Type: Free, Public
Diploma: Yes
Cost: Free
If free, where?: Within the county
Teen and/or Adult: Teens
Additional information: Hamilton County Virtual School offers 49 online courses. It is possible for students to become full-time students at HCVS, but they must withdraw from their home school.

Mansfield ISD Virtual School
Texas
United States
Tel: 817.299.6364
Web: www.misdvirtualschool.org
Email: PaulCash@misdmail.org
Recognition/Accreditation: Texas Education

Agency
Grade: 9-12
Type: Free, Public
Diploma: Yes
Cost: Free
If free, where?: Within the district
Additional information: Mansfield ISD Virtual School utilizes the Advanced Academics curriculum. The program is for students who are behind in their credits or for those who want to accelerate.

SBISD Academy of Choice Virtual High School
955 Campbell
Houston, Texas 77024
United States
Tel: 713.251.1500
Fax: 713.365.4226
Web: vhs.springbranchisd.com
Email: elearning@springbranchisd.com
Recognition/Accreditation: Spring Branch Independent School District
Grade: 9-12
Type: Public
Diploma: Yes
Cost: Free
If free, where?: Within the district
Additional information: If you are currently enrolled in an SBISD school, on-level and credit recover courses are free during the fall and spring. Summer courses are $200 per semester. Advanced Placement and Pre-AP courses are $100 per semester in fall and spring. These same courses are $350 per semester during the summer session.

Texas Virtual Academy
1800 Lakeway Drive
Suite 100
Lewisville, Texas 75057
United States
Tel: 866.360.0161
Web: www.K12.com/txva
Email: info@txva.org
Grade: 3-12
Type: Charter, Free, Public
Diploma: Yes
Cost: Free
If free, where?: Within the state
Teen and/or Adult: Teens
Additional information: Texas Virtual Academy utilizes the digital curriculum from K12, Inc. The school is in partnership with ResponsiveEd. It offers many extracurricular activities as well as an advanced learner program.

Electronic High School
250 East 500 South
PO Box 144200
Salt Lake, Utah 84114
United States
Tel: 801.538.7564
Fax: 801.538.7877
Web: www.schools.utah.gov/ehs/default.htm
Email: ehs@lists.uen.org
Recognition/Accreditation: NWAC
Grade: 9-12
Type: Free, Public
Diploma: Yes
Cost: Free
If free, where?: Within the state
Teen and/or Adult: Teens

130

Additional information: Most Electronic High School students use EHS classes only for supplemental credit and do not pursue a diploma from EHS. However, the Electronic High School offers a Utah diploma to a very restricted group of Utah students. See the website for details.

Mountain Heights Academy
9067 S. 1300 W. Suite 204
West Jordan, Utah
Tel: 801.721.6329
Web: mountainheightsacademy.org
Email: On website
Recognition/Accreditation: NAAS
Grade: 7-12
Type: Charter, Free, Public
Diploma: Yes
Cost: Free
If free, where?: Within the state
Teen and/or Adult: Teens
Additional information: "Eligible high school juniors and seniors can also participate in the Online Early Access program to earn both university and high school credit through Weber State University, Southern Utah University. Eligible 9-12 grade students have the option of earning credits by exam via Excelsior College."

Open High School of Utah
352 Denver Street Suite 350
Salt Lake, Utah 84110
United States
Tel: 801.721.6329
Fax: 888 .670.0032
Web: www.openhighschool.org
Email: info@openhighschool.org
Recognition/Accreditation: NWAC

Grade: 9-12
Type: Charter, Free, Public
Diploma: Yes
Cost: Free
If free, where?: Within the state
Teen and/or Adult: Teens
Additional information: Full-time and part-time programs are available. In order to be accepted, you must win a spot in their lottery.

Utah Virtual Academy
512 E. 4500 S., Suite 200
Murray, Utah 84107
United States
Tel: 801.262.4922 / 866.788.0364
Web: www.K12.com/utva/
Email: pglanton@K12.com
Recognition/Accreditation: Utah Department of Education
Grade: 1-12
Type: Charter, Free, Public
Diploma: No
Cost: Free
If free, where?: Within the state
Teen and/or Adult: Teens
Additional information: Utah Virtual Academy utilizes the digital curriculum from K^{12}, Inc. Loaner computers are available to students who need them. The school offers a variety of extracurricular activities and an advanced learners program.

Virtual Virginia
Virginia
United States
Tel: 804.786.9281
Web: www.virtualvirginia.org
Email: cathy.cheely@virtualvirginia.org

Recognition/Accreditation: Virginia Department of Education
Grade: 6-12
Type: Free, Public
Diploma: No
Cost: Free
If free, where?: Within the state
Teen and/or Adult: Teens
Additional information: Virtual Virginia (VVa) offers online Advanced Placement, world language, core academic, and elective courses to students around the country. While free for certain types of students, others will need to pay tuition. Check the website for additional information.

Explorer Academy
Washington
United States
Tel: 877.513.8977
Web: www.washingtononlineschool.com/explorer.html
Email: On website
Recognition/Accreditation: South Kitsap School District
Grade: 6-12
Type: Charter, Free, Public
Diploma: Yes
Cost: Free
If free, where?: Within the district
Teen and/or Adult: To age 21
Additional information: Explorer Academy uses curriculum provided by Advanced Academics. It accepts students under the age of twenty-one.

iConnect Academy
2001 26th Ave NE
Olympia, Washington 98506

United States
Tel: 360.596.7730
Fax: 360.596.7731
Web: orla.osd.wednet.edu/iconnect
Email: jwalton@osd.wednet.edu
Recognition/Accreditation: Olympia School District
Grade: 9-12
Type: Free, Public
Diploma: Yes
Cost: Free
If free, where?: Within the state
Teen and/or Adult: Teens
Additional information: iConnect Academy provides online courses to a number of school districts within Washington State. Instruction is conducted by a group of local teachers.

Insight School of Washington
12011 Bel-Red Road, Suite 101
Bellevue, Washington 98005
United States
Tel: 866.800.0017
Fax: 866.221.7831
Web: wa.insightschools.net
Email: info@insightwa.net
Recognition/Accreditation: NWAC
Grade: 9-12
Type: Charter, Free, Public
Diploma: Yes
Cost: Free
If free, where?: Within the state
Teen and/or Adult: Teens
Additional information: Insight School of Washington is part of the K12, Inc. family of online schools. It offers offer 120 courses including honors and Advanced Placement. It also offers students

vocational and skill-building online courses.

Internet Academy
31455 28th Ave S
Federal Way, Washington 98003
United States
Fax: 253.945.2233
Web: iacademy.org
Email: registrar@iacademy.org
Recognition/Accreditation: NWAC
Grade: 1-12
Type: Free, Public
Diploma: No
Cost: Free
If free, where?: Within the state
Teen and/or Adult: Teens
Additional information: Internet Academy was Washington's first online school. It offers both part-time and full-time options for students. In addition, Internet Academy provides parents with free parent-monitoring accounts to promote student success.

iQ Academy Washington
PO Box 8910
Vancouver, Washington 98668
United States
Tel: 888.899.4792
Fax: 888.827.1745
Web: iqacademywa.com
Email: info@iqacademywa.com
Recognition/Accreditation: Evergreen Public School District
Grade: 6-12
Type: Charter, Free, Public
Diploma: Yes
Cost: Free

If free, where?: Within the state
Teen and/or Adult: To age 21
Additional information: iQ Academy Washington is part of K12, Inc.'s family of schools. The school has both full-time and part-time programs available. In addition to the online curriculum, iQ Academy Washington uses weekly Elluminate sessions to provide additional instruction.

Kent Virtual High School
11000 SE 264 Street
Kent, Washington 98030
United States
Tel: 877.513.8977
Web: www1.kent.k12.wa.us/ksd/PH/kvhs.html
Email: michael.whitten@kent.k12.wa.us
Recognition/Accreditation: NWAC
Grade: 9-12
Type: Free, Public
Diploma: Yes
Cost: Free
If free, where?: Within the district
Teen and/or Adult: Teens
Additional information: Kent Virtual High School offers more than ninety online courses. Students have access to teachers through a variety of methods including instant messaging, email, fax, or telephone. The school's basic premise is that students learn differently and encourage students who need another option in order to be successful with their high school education.

Marysville Online Virtual Education
The Move Up program
Marysville, Washington
United States

Tel: 877.513.8977
Web: iwantograduate.com
Recognition/Accreditation: NCA
Grade: 9-12
Type: Free, Public
Diploma: Yes
Cost: Free
If free, where?: Within the state
Teen and/or Adult: To age 21
Additional information: Marysville Online Virtual Education, the MOVE UP program, utilizes digital curriculum from Advanced Academics. This program is for students who are looking for an alternative to the traditional classroom environment.

Puyallup Online Academy
Washington
United States
Tel: 877.513.8977
Web:
www.washingtononlineschool.com/puyallup.html
Email: On website
Recognition/Accreditation: Puyallup School District
Grade: 7-12
Type: Free, Public
Diploma: Yes
Cost: Free
If free, where?: Within the district
Teen and/or Adult: To age 21
Additional information: Puyallup Online Academy is part of the Washington Online School Network and it utilizes the digital curriculum provided by Advanced Academics. This program is for students who live with the Puyallup School District and who are interested in a full-time

program. Potential students for the Puyallup Online Academy must be under the age of twenty-one.

Selah Online

Washington
United States
Tel: 877.513.8977
Web:
www.washingtononlineschool.com/selah.html
Email: On website
Recognition/Accreditation: Selah School District
Grade: 7-12
Type: Free, Public
Diploma: Yes
Cost: Free
If free, where?: Within the district
Teen and/or Adult: Teens
Additional information: Selah Online is part of the Washington Online School Network and it utilizes the digital curriculum provided by Advanced Academics. Students must reside within the Selah School District. It is available to students in grades 8 – 12 and is available to full-time students.

Spokane Virtual Learning

2900 East 1st Avenue
Spokane, Washington 99202
United States
Tel: 509.354.7545
Fax: 509.354.7582
Web:
www2.spokaneschools.org/OnlineLearning/index.php
Email: SVL@SpokaneSchools.Org

Recognition/Accreditation: NWAC
Grade: 7-12
Type: Free, Public
Diploma: Yes
Cost: Free
If free, where?: Within the district
Teen and/or Adult: Teens
Additional information: Spokane Virtual Learning (SVL) is a Web-based educational project providing instructor-led online courses to students in Spokane Public Schools and across Washington State.

Twin Cities Virtual Academy
Washington
United States
Tel: 877.513.8977
Web: www.washingtononlineschool.com/twincities.html
Email: On website
Recognition/Accreditation: NCA, Partnering District
Grade: 7-12
Type: Free, Public
Diploma: Yes
Cost: Free
If free, where?: Within the district
Teen and/or Adult: Teens
Additional information: Twin Cities Virtual Academy is part of the Washington Online School Network. It is one of the largest virtual middle and high school networks in the Northwest. It is free within Chehalis and Centralia School Districts.

Vancouver Virtual Learning Academy
Washington
United States

Tel: 877.513.8977
Web: washingtononlineschool.com/vancouver.html
Email: On website
Recognition/Accreditation: Vancouver Public Schools
Grade: 6-12
Type: Free, Public
Diploma: Yes
Cost: Free
If free, where?: Southwest Washington
Teen and/or Adult: To age 21
Additional information: Vancouver Virtual Learning Academy is part of the Washington Online School Network and it utilizes the digital curriculum provided by Advanced Academics. Students must reside in Southwest Washington. Students must have at least a sixth grade reading level. Students must also be willing to attend a three-hour lab session each week.

Washington Online School Network
Washington
United States
Tel: 877.513.8977
Web: www.washingtononlineschool.com
Email:
Recognition/Accreditation: Washington Department of Education
Grade: 6-12
Type: Free, Public
Diploma: Yes
Cost: Free
If free, where?: Varies depending on network school
Teen and/or Adult: To age 21

Additional information: Washington Online School Network utilizes the Advanced Academics curriculum. It is a network of online schools throughout the state of Washington.

Washington Virtual Academies
1584 McNeil Street, Suite 200
DuPont, Washington 98327
United States
Tel: 253.964.1068
Fax: 253.964.1143
Web: www.K12.com/wava/
Email: info@wava.org
Recognition/Accreditation: NWAC
Grade: 1-12
Type: Charter, Free, Public
Diploma: Yes
Cost: Free
If free, where?: Within the state
Teen and/or Adult: Teens
Additional information: Washington Virtual Academies utilize the digital curriculum from K[12], Inc. It offers a variety of extracurricular activities and an advanced learners program for its students.

Yakima Online!
1120 South 18th Street
Yakima, Washington 98901
United States
Tel: 509.573.5580
Fax: 509.469.9045
Web: schools.yakimaschools.org/education/school/school.php?sectionid=7/
Recognition/Accreditation: NWAC
Grade: 9-12
Type: Free, Public

Diploma: Yes
Cost: Free
If free, where?: Within the district
Teen and/or Adult: Teens
Additional information: Yakima Online! Utilizes digital curriculum provided by Advanced Academics. This program is for students seeking an alternative to a traditional school classroom. The digital curriculum used by the school is competency-based.

Yelm Community Online School
Washington
United States
Tel: 877.513.8977
Web:
www.washingtononlineschool.com/yelm.html
Recognition/Accreditation: Yelm Community Schools District
Grade: 7-12
Type: Free, Public
Diploma: Yes
Cost: Free
If free, where?: Within the district
Teen and/or Adult: To age 21
Additional information: Yelm Community Schools Online utilizes the Advanced Academics curriculum. You must reside within the Yelm Community Schools District and have successfully completed at least the sixth grade.

West Virginia Virtual School
1900 Kanawha Boulevard, East Building 6, Room 346
Charleston, West Virginia 25305
United States
Tel: 304.558.7880 x. 53006

Web:
virtualschool.k12.wv.us/vschool/index.html
Email: atmeadow@access.k12.wv.us
Recognition/Accreditation: West Virginia
Department of Education
Grade: 1-12
Type: Free, Public
Diploma: No
Cost: Free
If free, where?: Within the state
Teen and/or Adult: Teens
Additional information: West Virginia Virtual
School is a project of the West Virginia Department
of Education. It uses online courses from a number
of different online providers. It presently has more
than 250 courses available. Typically, students take
courses at West Virginia Virtual School when a
course is not offered at their traditional school.

21st Century eSchool
7106 South Avenue
Middleton, Wisconsin 53562
United States
Tel: 608.829.9027
Web: www.mcpasd.k12.wi.us/our-schools-
0/other-options/21st-century-eschool
Email:
Recognition/Accreditation:
Grade: 1-12
Type: Free, Public
Diploma: Yes
Cost: Free
If free, where?: Within the district
Teen and/or Adult: Teens
Additional information: 21st Century eSchool is
part of the Middleton-Cross Plains Area School
District. The school is free for students in the

district. It utilizes the K¹², Inc. curriculum.

JEDI Virtual School
1221 Innovation Drive
Whitewater, Wisconsin 53563
United States
Tel: 262.473.1469
Fax: 608.868.4864
Web: www.jedivirtual.org
Email:
Recognition/Accreditation: Wisconsin
Department of Public Instruction
Grade: 1-12
Type: Charter, Free, Public
Diploma: Yes
Cost: Free for consortium districts
Teen and/or Adult: Teens
Additional information: JEDI Virtual School
provides each student with a Personal Education
Plan. This plan offers a comprehensive K-12
curriculum. The program is free to students in the
districts of Cambridge, Fort Atkinson, Jefferson,
Lake Mills, Marshall, Sun Prairie, and Whitewater.

Monroe Virtual High School
801 32nd Avenue
Monroe, Wisconsin 53566
United States
Tel: 888.947.6437
Fax: 608.328.7288
Web: www.virtualdiploma.net
Email: peggy.bahler@monroe.k12.wi.us
Recognition/Accreditation: NCA
Grade: 9-12
Type: Free, Public
Diploma: Yes
Cost: Free

If free, where?: Within the state
Teen and/or Adult: To age 21
Additional information: Monroe Virtual High School offers over 300 online courses. NVHS uses curriculum from a number of university-based online schools including Brigham Young University, the University of Missouri, and the University of Nebraska. It also uses courses from the North Dakota Center for Distance Education, and its own independent study courses.

West Bend Online Learning Academy
735 S. Main St.
West Bend, Wisconsin 53090
United States
Tel: 262.335.5459
Web: west-bend.k12.wi.us
Email: On website
Recognition/Accreditation: Wisconsin Department of Instruction
Grade: 9-12
Type: Free, Public
Diploma: No
Cost: Free
If free, where?: Within the district
Teen and/or Adult: Teens
Additional information: The West Bend School District has more than seventy online courses available. Laptop computers are available for check-out to students. West Bend Online Learning Academy offers both full-time and part-time programs.

Wisconsin Virtual Academy
4709 Dale-Curtin Drive
McFarland, Wisconsin 53558
United States

Tel: 608.838.9482
Fax: 608.838.9483
Web: www.K12.com/wiva/home
Email: info@wivcs.org
Recognition/Accreditation: McFarland School District
Grade: 1-12
Type: Charter, Free, Public
Diploma: Yes
Cost: Free
If free, where?: Within the state
Teen and/or Adult: Teens
Additional information: Wisconsin Virtual Academy (WIVA), a charter school authorized by the McFarland School District, utilizes the digital curriculum of K^{12}, Inc. The school issues laptop computers for use by all of their students.

Wyoming Connections Academy
1315 South US Highway, Suite 201 P.O. Box 15270
Jackson, Wyoming 83002
United States
Tel: 800.382.6010
Fax: 307.734.1314
Web: www.connectionsacademy.com/wyoming-school/home.aspx
Email: info@connectionsacademy.com
Recognition/Accreditation: AdvancED
Grade: 1-12
Type: Charter, Free, Public
Diploma: Yes
Cost: Free
If free, where?: Within the state
Teen and/or Adult: Teens
Additional information: Wyoming Connections Academy is part of the Connections Academy chain of schools. The school offers a wide variety of clubs

and activities. It provides students with free textbooks and laptop computers for home use.

Wyoming e-Academy of Virtual Education
90 Ethete Road
Fort Washakie, Wyoming 82520
United States
Tel: 307.332.0142
Fax: 307.335.8020
Web: www.fortwashakieschool.com/fwhs/
Recognition/Accreditation: NCA
Grade: 9-12
Type: Charter
Diploma: Yes
Cost: Free
If free, where?: Within the state
Teen and/or Adult: Teens
Additional information: This is a program with Fort Washakie Charter High School. Fort Washakie High School [FWHS] and the Wyoming e-academy of Virtual Education [WeAVE] provides high quality online learning options for students, teachers, school districts, and others involved in education for Wyoming students.

Index of Schools by State or Province

Clovis Online School
Delta Pacific Online
Dunlap Leadership Academy
Elk Grove Unified School District Virtual Academy
Golden State Virtual Academy
Golden Valley Virtual Charter School
iHigh Virtual Academy
Insight School of California - Los Angeles
Insight School of California - North Bay
iQ Academy California: Los Angeles
Juan Bautista de Anza Online Charter School
National University Academy
Pivot Online Charter School, North Bay
Pivot Online Charter School, North Valley
Pivot Online Charter School, Riverside
Pivot Online Charter School, San Diego
Riverside Virtual School
San Diego Virtual School
UC Online Academy
University of California College Prep

Colorado   61
Academy Online High School
Branson School Online
Colorado Connections Academy
Colorado Distance and Electronic Learning Academy
Colorado Virtual Academy
Denver Online High School
eDCSD / Colorado Cyber
HOPE Online Learning Academy Co-op
Insight School of Colorado
JeffCo's 21st Century Virtual Academy
Karval Online Education
Monte Vista On Line Academy
Provost Academy Colorado

North Carolina   109
North Carolina Virtual Public School

Ohio   110
Electronic Classroom of Tomorrow
iLearnOhio
Ohio Connections Academy
Ohio Distance & Electronic Learning Academy
Ohio Virtual Academy
QDA
TRECA Digital Academy
Virtual Community School of Ohio

Oklahoma   115
Oklahoma Virtual Charter Academy
Oklahoma Virtual High School
OSU K-12 Distance Learning Academy

Oregon   117
Clackamas Web Academy
Insight School of Oregon
Oregon Connections Academy
Oregon State University K-12 Online
Oregon Virtual Academy

Pennsylvania   121
21st Century Cyber Charter School
Achievement House Charter School
Agora Cyber Charter School
Commonwealth Connections Academy
PA Distance Learning Charter School
PA Learners Online
Pennsylvania Cyber Charter School
Pennsylvania Virtual Charter School
SusQ-Cyber Charter School

Internet Academy
iQ Academy Washington
Kent Virtual High School
Marysville Online Virtual Education
Puyallup Online Academy
Selah Online
Spokane Virtual Learning
Twin Cities Virtual Academy
Vancouver Virtual Learning Academy
Washington Online School Network
Washington Virtual Academies
Yakima Online!
Yelm Community Online School

West Virginia   146
West Virginia Virtual School

Wisconsin   146
21st Century eSchool
JEDI Virtual School
Monroe Virtual High School
West Bend Online Learning Academy
Wisconsin Virtual Academy

Wyoming   150
Wyoming Connections Academy
Wyoming e-Academy of Virtual Education

Author Information

In addition to being the author of *Complete Guide to Online High Schools* (2012) and *Best Online Christian Schools* (2014), Thomas Nixon is co-author of *Bears' Guide to Earning Degrees by Distance Learning* (2006) and of *Bears' Guide to the Best Education Degrees by Distance Learning* (2001).

Relevantly, he is also the author of *Bears' Guide to Earning High School Diplomas Nontraditionally* (2003) and is the manager of BestOnlineHighSchools.com and other online school websites. Yes, Tom really was that nerd that spent far too much time in high school looking at college catalogs. This early exposure has, apparently, molded him into a writer of college and high school guides.

Nixon coordinates online learning for Fresno Unified School District, the fourth largest district in California. He also teaches library media and educational technology courses in the School of Education at Fresno Pacific University.

He is the 2009 recipient of the California School Library Association's Innovation Award.

Tom can be contacted through his website, http://BestOnlineHighSchools.com or with his email at Tom@thomasnixon.com.

Other Books by Degree Press

Best Online Christian Schools (2014)

A brand new book from Degree Press! If you have ever considered attending an online school, but would like one that shares your Christian values, **Best Online Christian Schools** provides you with all of the information you need to make the right choice.

Get the comprehensive resource for Christian schools which have online programs when you purchase Best Online Christian Schools from Degree Press. This electronic book will provide you with all of the information that you need to know if you are planning to pursue an online high school education at a Christian school! The book is 53 Pages.

Get your copy of the Best Online Christian Schools and have it in your hands in just a few minutes!

Get it at DegreePress.com today!

Complete Guide to Online High Schools

You no longer have to sit in a traditional and, perhaps, boring classroom in order to earn a high school diploma. You no longer have to sit with students who are half your age. You no longer have to be tied to one geographical location. Online high schools are now an option for students of all ages and you can work at home or you can work on the road. These schools work well both for traditionally-aged high school students and for those who have more life experience.

In this second edition of **Complete Guide to Online High Schools: Distance learning options for teens and adults**, Thomas Nixon has expanded the offerings by showcasing almost triple the number of online high schools. Just as his Best Online High Schools website has grown over the years, so, too, has the size of this book.

Get it at DegreePress.com today!

California Online High Schools (2014)

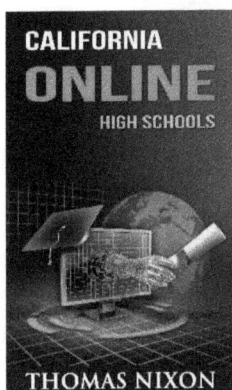

If you live in California and want to pursue an online High School Education in the State, this is the book that you need!

Get the comprehensive resource for Online High Schools in California when you purchase **California Online High Schools** from Degree Press. This electronic book will provide you with all of the information that you need to know if you are planning to pursue an online high school education in California! The book is 70 pages.

Get your copy of the California Online High Schools and have it in your hands in just a few minutes!

Get it at DegreePress.com today!

Colorado Online High Schools (2014)

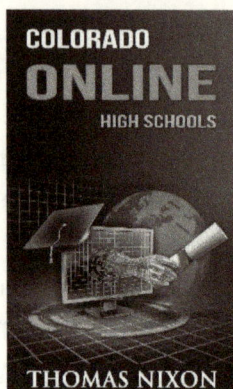

Washington Online High Schools (2014)

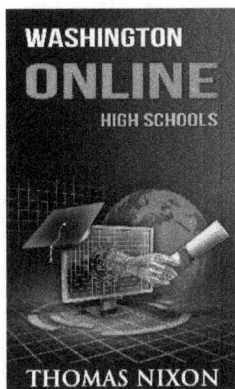

If you live in Washington and want to pursue an online High School Education in the State, this is the book that you need!

Get the comprehensive resource for Online High Schools in Washington when you purchase Washington Online High Schools from Degree Press. This electronic book will provide you with all of the information that you need to know if you are planning to pursue an online high school education in Washington! The book is 60 Pages.

Get your copy of the Washington Online High Schools and have it in your hands in just a few minutes!

Get it at DegreePress.com today!

Are you an online high school, but are not in this book?

Send an email to info@degreepress.com and let us know!

www.ingramcontent.com/pod-product-compliance
Lightning Source LLC
Chambersburg PA
CBHW032111280326
41933CB00009B/795